Data Driven

Data Driven

Profiting from Your Most
Important Business Asset

Thomas C. Redman

Harvard Business Press
Boston, Massachusetts

Library of Congress Cataloging-in-Publication Data

Redman, Thomas C.
 Data driven : profiting from your most important business asset / Thomas C. Redman.
    p. cm.
 ISBN 978-1-4221-1912-9
 1. Information resources management. 2. Organization. I. Title.
 T58.64.R43 2008
 658.4'038—dc22

                                                           2008022312

Contents

For Nancy; our dance continues

Acknowledgments

First, I need to thank Bell Labs and AT&T. Although AT&T bashing has been great sport for some time, people should recall that AT&T changed the world, a claim few companies can make. One of the best things it did was set up Bell Labs, its fabled research and development arm. I'll spare readers the long story, but suffice it to say that, for me, one fortuitous event led to another and I led a lab focused on data quality a full dozen years before most others even began to understand the importance of the issue. Indeed, all of AT&T was our lab, as we cantered back and forth working on specific AT&T problems and the underlying principles and methods.

I also need to thank my clients. Since leaving Bell Labs, I have had the privilege and pleasure of working with hundreds of people in dozens of companies from everywhere on the globe. Data have been relegated to a second tier for way too long, and these individuals and companies are blazing important trails. I especially admire the raw courage of those who have tried to make something happen in the face of pervasive organizational resistance.

I wish to thank several people whose fingerprints are all over this book. Blan Godfrey bears the dubious distinction of offering me my only full-time job, and he did it twice. Like me, Blan trained as a statistician at Florida State. Through his words and actions, he showed me that there are two types of statisticians: those who get out of their offices and those who do not. Those who do have a chance to contribute! Blan and I see each other every couple of years, and he never fails to charge me up. You couldn't ask for a better mentor.

After we had solved a number of specific problems at AT&T, we decided it was time to develop some underlying theory, and Anany Levitin led the charge. His first task was to sort through the haze and define *data*. As he completed that task, we realized that the effort completely missed the point! For to define data, we had to pin them down, looking at them as they sat in a database. But you cannot pin data down! They are alive, coming into being, flying from place to place, helping this person complete an operation and that person make a decision. This is a far more insightful way to view data. This big "Aha!" moment was the first time I thought we might be on to something special.

One of my first clients after I left Bell Labs was Jeff McMillan, and he and I have grown closer over the years. He has pushed me to create an "M-TOE" (Management Theory of Everything) that fully integrates data, technology, process, strategy, human resources, and anything else that is on our minds. Obviously this book is not that, but it is a darn sight broader than it would have been without Jeff's demands.

I have had the great pleasure of working with Bob Pautke and Dennis Parton for over twenty years. Dennis can see the essence of anything faster than anyone I have ever met. If Bob had a catchphrase, it would be "Embrace the politics." And I don't know how many times, when faced with a challenge or opportunity, I've asked myself, "How would Bob think about this?" or "How would Dennis think about this?"

A few people in each of thousands of places are struggling to help their organizations understand the importance of data. It is taking time, but we're making steady progress and, slowly, ushering in the true Information Age. Lwanga Yonke is trying to make their jobs easier. Some years ago he pointed out to me that everyone claimed they wanted to "manage data and information as assets," but it was just a sound bite. This comment helped shape this book.

I have greatly enjoyed working with Jacque Murphy, my editor at the Harvard Business Press. She was simultaneously demanding, encouraging, insightful, incisive, and patient. Best of all, she took the time to really understand why data are so important and work with me to craft a book that brings the most important topics to the fore.

I am a big believer in small-scale experiments, collecting and analyzing the data on practically anything. My family has endured thousands of such experiments, frequently with good humor. This is more important than it may first appear, because "data in the family" and "data in an enormous corporation" are strikingly similar! So thanks to my children and their spouses (Jenn and Joe; Andy and Liz; and Greg). In addition, Greg lent a real hand on a couple of key sections in the manuscript and proved himself a solid researcher

Finally, I must thank Nancy, my bride of thirty-one years. She demanded that a data geek (me) write a book about this esoteric stuff (data and information) that a regular person (her) could appreciate. And she made the work to get there fun.

Foreword

When I first met Tom Redman, I was terrified. He was bringing a mutual client to Morningstar, to assess our work as part of their supplier management program. While I was confident that our data quality was among the best—if not *the* best—in the industry, I was intimidated by Tom's credentials and knew that he might nail us in his review.

Here on our doorstep was someone who called himself the Data Doc; someone with a PhD and Bell Labs experience (the height of research excellence, in my mind); and someone who invented and led the Data Quality Lab from 1987 to 1995. He'd founded a successful consulting business, Navesink Consulting, and had organized a group of like-minded individuals into the International Association of Information and Data Quality. This group puts on a fantastic conference annually and you'll be impressed by the names of the companies that attend— Nike, Nestlé, IBM, Eli Lilly and Co., Toyota Motor Sales, Inc., Exxon-Mobil, Wyeth Pharmaceutical, and many more. He'd also authored a number of books on data quality. He really knew his stuff, and he knew our industry. And here he was in our office to assess our work.

Data is central to everything we do at Morningstar, and from the beginning we've known that we could build and grow an outstanding business if our data were of the highest quality, a quality that enables us to create informed, accurate analyses to help investors. In fact, we knew we'd never get anywhere if our clients didn't have the utmost confidence in our underlying data; when asked to choose the most important attributes of the company, they have always told us that data completeness and accuracy were their top purchasing criteria. As president of

Morningstar's Data Services business, I'm responsible for building and maintaining the databases that power all our products worldwide. We've seen day in and day out how great data can drive sales and how mistakes can cause expensive, time-consuming issues.

The good news is that we passed Tom's review—but we had more work to do. His book really captures what he told us then: that we all need to think about our data (and our customers) differently. How can you think about data differently? Facts are facts, right? Most people might not associate data, not to mention data quality, with creativity. As Tom describes it, data are "facts" (the quotes are his), but the creative part comes from what we do with those facts. While we may leverage our data itself to earn revenue, that's not ultimately the original motive for collecting the data. We collect investment data at Morningstar, for example, so that we can produce research and tools to help investors make better choices. And, obviously, we can only do this well if we pay attention to the quality of our data.

If you're looking for a book to get you excited about data, this is it. While Tom is well versed in all the details and could have written a very technical book, he has aimed this one at us generalist business types. The most valuable gift of this book is that it is a nontechnical journey through a very technical topic. And although it's not a "how to" book, the examples here are detailed enough to help you drive change in the way your company handles data. As Tom exhorts us, don't leave your data to IT; make it a key tool to driving your revenue and profits.

The happy and profitable "by-product" of collecting data (so that we can do something with it) is that the data itself becomes a moat around our business and gives us a unique competitive advantage. One of my favorite quotes from Tom's book characterizes this perfectly: "When you think about it for a minute it strikes you. Organizations are increasingly sophisticated at technology deployment, financial controls, and process management. The marginal returns from further investments are small. Investments in data are quite the opposite. The opportunities are limitless. And, more importantly, any investment you make is proprietary to your business. This is the true definition of competitive advantage."

I particularly like the case Tom makes for the continuous growth in demand for data. As he sees it, demand for data and information has been growing for hundreds of years and will only continue to grow. I can certainly see evidence of this in the investment industry. With the continuous invention of new investment vehicles alone, the demand for investment data will rise—not to mention the increasing education and sophistication of investors.

A common quality of successful investors is the steadfast ability to think independently. Read this book with a questioning mind. Challenge Tom's thinking. If there's even the smallest notion in your mind that the key to growing your business is data, either data about your business or turning the data you generate in the course of running your business into a "product" and selling it, you will find inspiration and utility in this book. Use it as a road map for bringing your data to market, clarifying your capabilities, and even finding the sweet spot in the market for your data. You'll learn hands-on the guiding principles that will shape the way you manage your company's data. Although no one can guarantee success, if you apply the precepts in this book and think for yourself, you'll be well on your way.

—*Liz Kirscher*
President, Data Services
Morningstar, Inc.

Data Are Business Assets

Savvy managers know that their futures, and that of their organization, depend on data and information. They know that data are crucial to everything they do, from understanding customers to developing a product and setting a direction. They sense that data and information are not just "the lifeblood of the Information Age," but the means by which they distance themselves from their competitors. Indeed, they realize that the stakes are so high that data and information must be treated as strategic assets. Smart managers want in.

However, managers are frustrated because their organizations do not pay data and information their due. Most data sit unused, with opportunities to create new products, identify new niches, and craft better strategies completely ignored. Few organizations can answer even the most basic questions about their data, such as "How much do you have?" or "What are they worth?" Even worse, data are incorrect, out-of-date, poorly defined, and otherwise unfit for action. They plague all of us and every organization—increasing costs, angering customers, and compromising decisions. Worst of all, bad data lie at the root of issues of international importance, including the current subprime mortgage meltdown, lost and stolen identities, hospital errors, and contested elections.

What to do?

This book aims to help answer that question. It is based on my experiences over the last thirty years. Trained as a statistician, I started my career at Bell Labs. I led a lab focused on data quality a full ten years before others even acknowledged the issue. In some ways, my "lab" was all of AT&T. My colleagues and I worked arm in arm with AT&T managers on data issues where, quite literally, billions were at stake. Then it was back to Bell Labs to try to figure out why various solutions did or did not work.

In 1996 I opened Navesink Consulting Group, and since then I've worked with dozens of organizations from a variety of industries and with hundreds of people up and down and across the organization chart. Almost all of these organizations have been leaders in their fields. I've had the pleasure of working on every continent except Africa, but the United States is overrepresented. So too are financial services, perhaps because the connections between data and money are so clear. The people I've worked with have possessed the rare traits of both strong internal visions of a better way to do things and the courage to try something new. This book summarizes what these pioneering souls and I have learned along the way.

Some of the lessons seem stunningly obvious in retrospect. For example, "If you want to reap the benefits of data and information as strategic assets, then you should manage them as aggressively and professionally as you do other assets" seems almost trite. But it is an important point that all too often gets lost in the din of day-in, day-out work. Potent though they are, data and information are not endowed with magical properties. Left alone, they do not tell managers how to leverage them in the market. They do not lead managers to make the right decisions. An incorrect datum cannot correct itself, or even warn people of the dangers of using it.

A second, less obvious, point is that the business side of the organization must lead the heavy lifting needed to manage data and information assets. This lesson may seem counterintuitive, given the enormous investments in information technologies over the last two generations. But all the really interesting and value-adding roles that data play occur in operations, product development, customer interactions, decision making, strategic planning, and other business departments. These areas also bear the brunt of the pain caused by data that are just plain wrong. And only they can eliminate the root causes of the underlying issues.

This book is therefore written for business managers, with four interrelated goals in mind:

- To help them get started, by providing some simple, pragmatic first steps, no matter what their level or position.

- To help them craft midterm plans, by showing how the daunting task of fully managing data and information assets can be broken down into more manageable chunks of work.

- To help them think long term, by introducing them to the mysteries of data and information. It is these mysteries that make data and information both so potentially valuable and so dangerous, and they reflect themselves in subtle, beautiful, and unique ways in each organization.

- To help them create a renewed urgency regarding data and information within their organizations. The potential and the hype are real. Entirely new strategies, products, and customers await. The flip side is that these opportunities await your competitors, known and unknown, as well.

Managing Data and Information Assets

In practice, managing data and information assets boils down to three deceptively simple actions. First, organizations must provide for the "care and feeding" of their data and information, just as they do for their capital and people assets. They strive to keep the right amount of cash on hand, invest in physical plant, and take steps to ensure that inventory does not walk away. They try to hire enough people with the right skill sets, place them in the right jobs, and nurture leaders.

For data and information, better care is mostly about quality. Organizations must correctly create or otherwise obtain the data and information they really need, correctly, the first time. They must make it easy for their people to find, access, and understand them, so people trust and use them with confidence and power. Finally, organizations must take reasonable steps to protect their data and information from being stolen or used in inappropriate ways.

Relatively few organizations could credibly claim to meet these criteria today, and most accounting systems do not capture the resulting costs and risks, which are enormous. Fortunately, however, relatively small investments to improve data and information quality pay impressive returns. The successes of Information Resources, Morningstar, and Interactive Data, whose data must pass market scrutiny every day, attest to the importance and power of high-quality data.

Second, organizations must put their (high-quality) data and information to work in unique and significant ways. They must embed data and information in the day-to-day running of the organization, employ them creatively to make better decisions, and leverage them to create and bring new products and services to market. They must think long term, identifying the data and information they *will need*, in effect integrating their data and business strategies. In other words, organizations must make data and information part and parcel of the organization's present and future.

Companies such as Netflix, Harrah's Casino, and the Oakland A's— "analytics competitors" in Tom Davenport and Jeanne Harris's terms— meet this criterion, and others are trying.[1] Yet too many companies do not fully exploit their data and information. Their approach is half-hearted and chaotic and their execution undisciplined. They do not seem to realize that people, as both consumers in their private lives and decision makers at work, have unquenchable thirsts for data and information. And not just for any data, but for *exactly the right data and information in exactly the right place at the right time and in the right format to complete an operation, serve a customer, make a decision, or set and execute strategy.*

There are many ways to bring data and information to market and reap the rewards of quenching some of this thirst. Morningstar does it through content, and Netflix through analytics. The capital-intensive container shipping industry provides a third example. By 2010 it is estimated that half of the value in the delivery of a container, from perhaps halfway across the globe, will be in the delivery of data and information associated with that container.[2] The shipping industry must "informationalize" container transport to deliver this value.

Organizations must fully embrace the potential; learn how to make better, more confident, and more *informed* decisions; tune into growing needs for data and information; and accelerate work to bring them to market. At this point, managers may feel encouraged because these first two prescriptions parallel their efforts for other assets. But it is not nearly so simple, because data and information have properties that present both opportunities and perils unlike any other asset. The most obvious, but far from most important, is that data and information can be shared, and to an almost limitless degree. Departments compete for the organization's investment dollar. If product development gets one, then operations does not. Not so with data and information. Marketing can use customer data to work out a rewards program at the same time that engineering is using them to design a product upgrade and sales is revamping its territories. This is one reason that data and information are potentially so valuable. The flip side is that it is more difficult to protect data and information from theft. The hundreds of incidents and millions of customer records compromised in recent years bear witness to this point.[3]

Data and information have many such properties that, collectively, present unparalleled opportunities and daunting challenges. Today's organizations are singularly ill-suited to these opportunities and challenges. Ask most organizations who is in charge of their data and they'll reply, "Our chief information officer." But far too many are really CTOs, where the *T* stands for "technology." They have no influence on bringing data and information to market and little influence on quality. Although they may well define and implement ever-larger databases that make the sharing of data and information technically feasible, they are singularly ill-positioned to convince people and departments that do not want to share their hard-earned data with others to do so.

The result is that data and information are essentially unmanaged assets. To address this issue, organizations must develop deep understandings of data and information, their eclectic properties, where they come from, how they move around, and the myriad ways in which they help create—and destroy—value. They must extend their management systems to accommodate and exploit these strange and wonderful properties.

The Time Is Now!

I am not, of course, the first to note the importance of data and information. They have always been important, even pivotal, for an elite few. Those with the best data have won wars, uncovered wholly new product spaces, and achieved insights into keeping costs low. Because data are central to the scientific method, they have played an essential role in virtually every advance for thousands of years.

But only now is the time right for data and information to enter the mainstream in most businesses. We would neither contemplate the vast market potential, worry about quality, nor notice the strange properties of data and information were it not for the stunning advances in information technology (IT) over the past two generations. Since the 1960s, organizations have devoted ever-increasing resources to IT. Figure I-1 depicts one aspect of this growth. These investments have paid off handsomely. It is impossible to overstate the importance of computers to the modern organization. None could survive, much less thrive, without various computing, storage, networking, and applications technologies.

Yet a provocative article entitled "IT Doesn't Matter" by Nicholas Carr suggests that the days of IT's strategic ascendancy are drawing to a close.[4] Carr points out that organizations cannot sustain advantage based on "infrastructure technologies," such as the electric grid and railroads.

FIGURE I-1

Percentage of capital expenditures devoted to IT by American companies

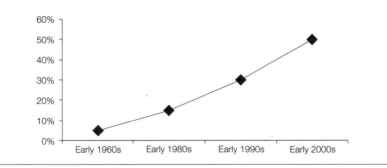

Early in the last century, companies that exploited the newly discovered electric power could obtain a measure of advantage. But that advantage evaporated when cheap electricity became available to all from the nearest outlet. Sustained advantage, Carr argues, stems from "proprietary technologies," such as a drug patent, a unique process that is hard to copy, or deep, tacit knowledge in a given area. Information technologies, however, be they databases, networks, or sophisticated application software, are rapidly becoming commodities, available to all for a fraction of their costs just a few years ago.

With respect to the subject of this book, these technologies enable organizations to routinely:

- Acquire and store vast quantities of data and information

- Deliver them from one place to another

- Process them to complete the organization's basic transactions

- Manipulate them to create new data and information better suited to specific tasks

Data and information are almost ready to be put to work in unique and significant ways. But lost in the headlong rush to implement the new technologies was any real concern about quality. The earliest computerphiles recognized the problem. They coined the now-famous expression "Garbage in, garbage out" to describe the situation and, I suspect, to deflect criticism from their systems when they returned useless answers. Unacceptably low data quality has come home to roost.

These observations lead us to expect the Information Age to unfold in three broad, overlapping, but distinct phases (figure I-2):

1. A coherent IT infrastructure, or IT buildout, phase[5]

2. A data quality phase

3. An exploiting data and information phase

Although there may be many loose ends to tidy up, organizations should, by now, be nearing the end of the first phase. Those that are should turn their attention to phase 2. Those that are not yet nearing the end of phase 1 should do so as quickly as possible.

FIGURE I-2

Phases of the Information Age

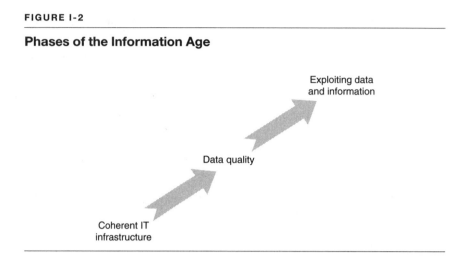

The quality phase corresponds to the "care and feeding" prescription outlined previously. Organizations should strive, for example, to improve data accuracy by one to two orders of magnitude and reduce the costs of poor data quality by up to two-thirds. The quality phase also paves the way for the third phase.

The exploiting data and information phase corresponds to the "put data and information to work" prescription. All organizations should begin thinking about this phase because there will be many tough issues to address. Those that feel their data can withstand market scrutiny should begin to test the waters.

This three-phase model does not explicitly mention the "advance the management system" prescription, although it is implied by each phase.

Plan for the Book

I hope that managers and organizations find these prescriptions, the claim that demands for data and information are unquenchable, and the model of a three-phase Information Age provocative, stimulating, and useful. I'll build on these ideas throughout.

Chapter 1, "The Wondrous and Perilous Properties of Data and Information in Organizations," is in some respects the heart and soul of this book, because the special properties of data and information both endow them with great potential and make them difficult to harness. Most significant is that each organization's data and information are uniquely its own. Your competitor's dollar is exactly the same as yours, and he or she can steal your most valuable employees. Not so your data and information. They are all yours, to leave moldering away in databases or to use in novel ways inside your organizations and in your markets.

Part I focuses on quality. Chapter 2, "The (Often Hidden) Costs of Poor Data and Information," might be better entitled "The Cold, Brutal Reality." It focuses on the current state of data and information quality in the typical organization. There have been many examples in which bad data and information became front-page news, threatening organizations and executives. Fortunately, most cases of bad data don't make the paper. But most organizations have a lot of work to do to make their data and information fit for use.

If chapter 2 lays out the bad news, chapter 3, "Assessing and Improving Data Quality," lays out the good. It describes how three companies whose data must endure the rigors of the marketplace think about and address data quality. Not surprisingly, Morningstar, Interactive Data, and Tele-Tech Services invest their data quality efforts toward preventing errors at their sources. Chapter 3 features a maturity model that enables managers to baseline their organization's current data quality efforts. The case studies were specifically selected to help managers select first steps in advancing from that baseline.

Chapters 4 through 6 constitute part II. They focus on putting data and information to work. Chapter 4, "Making Better Decisions," looks at decision making through the data and information lens, providing insights that can help managers, and perhaps more importantly entire organizations, make better decisions.

Whereas chapter 4 focuses on one way to exploit data and information inside the organization, chapters 5 and 6 shift attention outside, to the marketplace. Lest there be any doubt, I have unbridled excitement that demands for "exactly the right data and information . . ." will grow without end. I have no less excitement about the variety of approaches for meeting those demands. Chapter 5 focuses on *content providers*, those who bring data and information directly to market. I've already cited two of six ways to do so, namely, providing new content and informationalization. Chapter 5 also aims to help potential content providers determine what is best for them. Chapter 6 discusses *facilitators*, those who help others find and use data and information more effectively.

Part III is aimed at advancing the management system for data and information. As data and information grow more important, in parallel, they grow more political. For example, some managers, fearing the loss of their fiefdoms, seek to control them. Similarly, privacy rights are in constant flux, making it unclear which uses of data and information are out of bounds. Chapter 7, "Social Issues in the Management of Data and Information," focuses on these issues with the intent of getting them out in the open.

The political issues of chapter 7 arise, in part anyway, because data and information are essentially unmanaged. In time, I believe that organizations will recognize that data and information merit special attention as assets in their own right and name true C-band chief data officers. But the C-suite is already too crowded, and for most organizations, the time is not yet right. Therefore, the focus of chapter 8, "Evolving the Management System for Data and Information," is on relatively simple steps that are proving their mettle today.

The prescriptions presented herein are demanding. Chapter 9, "The Next One Hundred Days," thus proposes a panoramic study of a horizontal slice of a business as a way to get started, gain some experience with the mysteries of data and information, baseline oneself against the practices and recommendations herein, and identify steps for moving forward.

CHAPTER ONE

The Wondrous and Perilous Properties of Data and Information in Organizations

Savvy managers recognize that data and information are strategic assets, possibly even the "ultimate proprietary technology," in Nicholas Carr's terms.[1] After all, they are the only asset that is uniquely your own. No other organization has, or can have, the same data that your organization has. Your data reflect your strategies, customers, products, employees—everything that matters in your organization. Competitors can copy your processes, buy the same equipment you do, steal your customers, and entice your employees with better offers. But unless you let them, they can't have your data and information.

Further, data and information have properties and play roles in organizations that have no good analogues in other assets. I cited sharing in the introduction, but data and information are not endowed with some sort of "sharing gene." Rather, they can be digitized, copied, and transported at extremely low cost. It is these properties that make them shareable and in turn offer the potential for people and departments to work together for leverage across the organization and to help management get everyone on the same page. Not without a price, however: these same properties also make it possible, in a careless moment, for the bad guys to steal your data without you even knowing it.

Data and information possess many properties that simultaneously promise enormous potential and pose unprecedented challenges. Managers must become adept at finding courses of action that take advantage of the upside and avoid the downside.

Data Multiplies

Ask any executive, in practically any industry or role, how much data his or her department has and you will likely get a short answer: "Tons. We have tons of data!" The reason is quite simple. All activities that use data create more in the process. Taking a customer order creates new data. So does making the next widget. So too financial reporting. Every operation, every decision, every strategic action—all create more data.

Estimates of the *doubling time* (the time it takes the quantity of an organization's data to double) vary from twelve to eighteen months.[2] Take a typical doubling time of one year. If the organization currently stores one terabyte, it will store two terabytes a year from now, and four and eight terabytes two and three years from now, respectively. Impressive, but the most compelling statement is from Lou Gerstner, who as chairman of IBM remarked, "Inside IBM, we talk about 10 times more connected people, 100 times more network speed, 1,000 times more devices, and a million times more data."[3]

Contributing to the explosion, organizations also acquire vast quantities of data from outside their borders. Most come into the organization through everyday commerce with customers, suppliers, and regulators. Other data are purchased. For example, the financial services industry is heavily dependent on market data provided by Bloomberg, Interactive Data, Morningstar, and others. Marketing departments in many industries purchase demographic data from Acxiom, ChoicePoint, and Dun & Bradstreet.

It is not just the quantities of data that are increasing; so too are the types of data. Only a few years ago, few would have foreseen the penetration of global positioning systems and the data they spawn. Or the human genome. Or radio frequency identification.

The upside is potentially enormous. First and foremost, the data you create are uniquely your own. And you create more every day. More data, in greater variety and detail, means there are more data to mine, more ways to informationalize, and more angles from which to view a problem. More insights into your competitor's intentions and novel twists can help you make better decisions.

The downside is that managers are already buried in data and the problem is growing worse. "More" does not imply "more really good stuff," although it usually does imply that the task of sifting through the mass of data to find what you really need is larger and more complex. And "more" means that greater management attention is needed regarding both the internal and external sources of all these data. A bit more subtly, "more" also means a lot more time and effort figuring out how the data obtained from different sources relate to one another.

To get in front of this onslaught, managers and organizations must determine which data are most important and focus their efforts. I find that it is often easier, although somewhat less effective, to determine which data are never used for anything and to stop collecting them.

Data Are More Complex Than They Appear

Henry Petroski uses paper clips to illustrate the complexity of today's world. Paper clips are so simple, basic, and inexpensive that they almost escape notice. But so many specialized disciplines must come together to make a paper clip that he doubts any human knows all there is to know about manufacturing one.[4] Like a paper clip, a datum may seem simple, basic, and inexpensive, yet it is surprisingly complex. And also like a paper clip, many disciplines must come together if even the simplest datum is to prove useful. These include the following:

- Data modeling, which is essentially the process of specifying what you want. Often surprisingly abstract and technical, the process includes defining the entities, attributes, and relationships of interest, assembling these into databases, optimizing performance, and creating needed metadata (see "Data and Information Defined").

- Obtaining the data values via the organization's business processes or suppliers or both.

Data and Information Defined

There are many approaches to defining data. I find the one that best reflects how data are created and used in organizations most effective. In it, "data" consist of two components: a data model and data values. *Data models* are abstractions of the real world that define what the data are all about, including specifications of the things of interest (called *entities* in data lingo), important properties of those things (*attributes* or *fields* in the lingo), and relationships between them. As an example, an employee is an entity. His or her employer is interested in all its EMPLOYEES (an example of an *entity class* in the lingo), and attributes such as NAME, DEPARTMENT, SALARY, and MANAGER. REPORTS TO is an example of a relationship between two entities.

The Internal Revenue Service is also interested in the employee, as a TAXPAYER. It is interested in some of the attributes that interest the employer, but also in many others, such as INTEREST INCOME, that do not. The employee is, quite obviously, the same person, but each organization has distinct needs and interests, so their data models are different.

On its own, a data model is much like a blank meeting calendar: there is a structure, but no content. *Data values* complete the picture. They are assigned to attributes for specific entities. Thus, a single datum takes the form

<John Doe, DEPARTMENT = Research>

Here, John Doe is the entity, DEPARTMENT is the attribute, and Research is the department to which John Doe is assigned. *Data* are any collection of datum items of this form.

One last point on data. Clearly data, defined this way, are abstract. We do not actually see or touch them. What we actually see when we work with data are *data records*, which come in an almost unlimited number of forms: paper, computer applications, tables, charts, and so on. The practical importance is that the same data can be presented in many different ways. Choosing the right way to present the data is often as important as selecting the right data.

There are also many approaches to defining information. I find it most powerful to define information not in terms of what it *is*, but in terms of what it *does*. To illustrate, suppose you are playing a game of chance with one die. You bet a dollar and select a number, 1 to 6. A dealer then rolls a die, and you either lose your bet or are paid six dollars. You do not get to see the roll. Your chances of winning are roughly one in six, assuming the game is fair. Now consider the following "information" about the next roll:

Scenario A: Someone tells you that the die is loaded and the next roll will come up odd. You will pick 1, 3, or 5, and your chances of winning increase to one in three. You have been informed.

Scenario B: Someone tells you that the die is loaded and will come up odd when it will really come up even. You have been misinformed.

Scenario C: Someone tells you that the dealer is spinning a roulette wheel, not rolling a die. Your chances of winning are greatly reduced, but your understanding of the game comes closer to reality. You will almost certainly try to withdraw your bet. You have been informed.

Scenario D: Someone tells you that the die is red. Nothing changes. You have been neither informed nor misinformed.

Information, then, teaches you about the world. Sometimes it does so by reducing your uncertainty about future events, and other times by enlarging your perspective.[5]

Two subtleties are frequently important. First, although information can indeed be derived from data, it can arise in other ways as well. A train whistle that warns you of an approaching train is certainly informative, but it is hardly a datum. This book uses the catchall term *signals* to refer to data, train whistles, and anything else that may be informative. Second, information is intensely personal. For example, the person standing next to you, having seen the approaching train, might view the whistle as an annoying blast, not information.

- Recording the data, which involves putting them in the desired place and form, such as on a company database, a laptop computer, in a special paper file, or even a scrap of paper. (*Note:* One could make the case that facts filed in a person's head count as data, but memory is too ephemeral to qualify as a valid data record.)

- Selecting, finding, and accessing the right data needed to complete the specific operation or answer the question at hand.

- Presenting data in ways that make it easy for customers to understand and use them. Only in this last step do data and information contribute to internal operations and decisions or come to market.

Thus, like paper clips, data are more complex than they may first appear. This complexity means there are many different ways to make your data uniquely your own and, in so doing, make imitation more difficult. The flip side is that many activities have to go right. Any foul-ups and the data may be completely useless. Further, different people, often in different departments, complete the five jobs just listed. Savvy managers realize that excellence in all five departments is necessary but not sufficient. The work must be coordinated toward a common end.

Data and Information Are Subtle and Nuanced and Have Become the Organization's Lingua Franca

One of the first things schoolchildren learn is that each subject has its own special language. They learn about *themes* in English class, *square roots* in math, and *atoms* in science. Some terms are common—a *final* is the same everywhere. It is only natural that the same thing occurs in business as well. Retailers use the terms *SKU* and *UPC* to refer to products. A SKU is a "stock-keeping unit" and refers to an internal numbering system, whereas UPC is the "Universal Product Code" and refers to an external numbering system set up and administered by the Global Data Synchronization Network. SKUs and UPCs aim to make it easier for merchants and their suppliers to keep track of the items they sell.

Thus, it is only natural that highly technical data such as SKUs come to be used in the everyday business discourse in retail.

This phenomenon occurs everywhere. People in financial services call securities *CUSIPs*, those in shipping refer to *40-foot equivalents*, and people in travel recall the *fare-basis* without missing a beat. Over time, the language of a business becomes so much a part of their everyday lives that people no longer recognize that their terms are specialized. People who work in financial services just assume, for example, that everyone knows what a CUSIP is. It is difficult for them to explain the term to the uninitiated.

Data modelers capture this everyday language in defining an organization's data structures (the entities, attributes, and relationships described in the box above), which are then implemented in databases and computer applications. New people learn the language of the organization when they are taught how to use the system. In time, it is impossible to distinguish between everyday business language and data. Data have thus become a sort of organizational lingua franca. It is another way in which your data are uniquely your own. Figure 1-1 depicts the entire process.

Data, like the business language they reflect, have subtle meanings. Consider yourself as a "customer" of your doctor, financial adviser, lawyer, and an Internet retailer. To your doctor, you are a *patient*; to your financial adviser, an *account*; to your lawyer, a *client*; and to the retailer, a *shopper*—different terms reflecting subtly different relationships, with a special language and data for each. As figure 1-2 illustrates, even though there is some overlap, the "data about you" captured by your various "suppliers" are very different, and one collection will not serve another's needs. Further, data specifically designed for your doctor and financial adviser make each more effective and efficient.

And here, we come to the heart of this book. Just as doctors, financial advisers, lawyers, and retailers tailor data to their needs, *companies within an industry* can design their data differently than their competitors. For example, a retail bank may organize its data around an *individual*, a *couple*, or a *household*, based on its customer strategy. Some "data about you" will be common, but much will be very different. This nuance, subtlety, and intimate connection to everyday language are one major reason that each organization's data are uniquely its own.

FIGURE 1-1

Language and data

Everyday business language is captured, via data modeling, in an organization's data-bases and systems. These systems are often the means by which new employees learn. They may also include new terms, which in time become part of everyday business language.

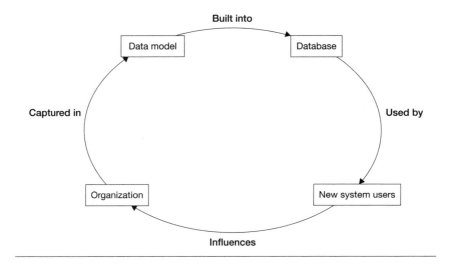

In the same way, data will be shaped within each department of a company. For example, at the retailer, customer service representatives view you as the *shopper*. But the order fulfillment department does not care a whit about your tastes or preferences. There, a shopper is nothing more than an address to which it sends the package. And marketing, recognizing that the Internet makes it easier for you to buy gifts for your spouse, may recognize him or her as the real shopper. Each department uses the term *shopper* in the way that best suits its purposes. This is, of course, just how it should be. Each department should evolve the means, including the associated language and data, to do its work effectively and efficiently.

The flip side is that cross-departmental communication is much more difficult. One of the most brutal battles I have witnessed revolved around the definition of *market share*. Two departments measured mar-

FIGURE 1-2

Diverse definitions of data

Data are subtle and nuanced. The column labels represent personal data about any individual. The row labels are various organizations that define and use data about individuals. There is some overlap, but each organization can define data to suit its specific needs.

Used by	Name	Address	Phone number	Credit card number	Credit card expiration	Age	Height and weight	House value	Investable income
Doctor	▓	▓	▓			▓	▓		
Financial adviser	▓	▓	▓			▓		▓	▓
Retailer	▓	▓	▓	▓	▓				

ket share at different points in the supply chain and, not surprisingly, obtained different results. The ensuing battle over "whose numbers were right" only stopped when a young analyst pointed out that the two sides were talking about different things.

This problem reflects itself in many ways. As Jeff McMillan of Merrill Lynch Research points out, many organizations complain that "our systems don't talk to each other when the real problem is that departments define things differently."[6] They fall into the trap of confusing a communications issue with a technology issue.

Figure 1-3 sums up these issues and opportunities. There is no one-size-fits-all resolution, although the following guidelines are helpful:

- Managers should strive for greater nuance and subtlety in data that are central to an organization's business strategies, most important market niches, and any area where the organization must distinguish itself from its competitors.

- Managers should strive for greater standardization in areas where communications are essential.

The large middle ground is problematic.

FIGURE 1-3

Summary of the opportunities and difficulties that stem from greater nuance and standardization in defining data

	Departmental efficiency	Cross-departmental communication	Systems development	Marketplace value
More nuanced, subtly defined	Higher	More difficult	More difficult	Higher value in fewer uses
More standardized	Lower	Easier	Easier	Lower value in more uses

Data and Information Create Value When They Are on the Move

Data sitting untouched in the most technologically sophisticated database may have a lot of potential. So too does a deep insight in a management report. But neither actually helps create any value until it is used. Just the opposite, in fact. Data and information are most valuable when they are flying from place to place, helping complete a customer order here, contributing to a management report there, and stirring a new idea in someone's mind somewhere else (see "The Data and Information Lens"). It is easier to get your arms around data when they are standing still, but doing so misses the point.

The concept of data on the move merits a detailed example, summarized in figure 1-4. The example begins with Sue talking to a customer service representative at a hypothetical company, Sweaters R Us. She wants to get her granddaughter Emily, who is about to turn sixteen, a teal, v-neck, medium-size sweater. The sweater is a present, and the package must arrive by the 27th of this month.

Now follow the data: first, the customer service representative must find Sue in "his system," check inventory, obtain Sue's credit card number, explain Sue's delivery options, obtain her granddaughter's name and address, and determine what the card enclosed with the sweater should say.

Order fulfillment, accounts receivable, and accounts payable all act on the data from Sue's order. Order fulfillment takes the sweater from stock, packages it, prints and encloses the card, applies the address label, and makes delivery arrangements. In doing so, it updates data about Sue and inventory. Accounts receivable collects payment and updates Sue's record. Accounts payable pays the sweater supplier and the delivery company, updating more data in the process.

Sue's data are also put to higher-level uses. Inventory management uses these data to help decide whether it is time to order more teal, v-neck, medium-size sweaters. Finance aggregates Sue's data with other data for reporting purposes. Marketing uses them to determine whether it should run a sweater sale, whether teal really has become more popular than aqua, and whether younger customers really do prefer the v-neck to the scoop neck.

The list of places Sue's data alight could go on and on. I'll give just one more. Sweaters R Us made a strategic decision some years ago to move its customers onto the Internet. It has invested millions in designing, testing, and implementing a customer-friendly Web site, and it has invested millions more advertising the site and training customers to use

The Data and Information Lens

I find looking at an organization through the data and information lens to be extremely powerful. To do so, one examines the movement and management of data and information as they wind their way across the organization. The lens reveals who touches them, how people and processes use them to add value, how they change, the politics surrounding seemingly mundane issues such as data sharing, how the data come to be fouled up, what happens when they are wrong, and so forth. There is simply no better way to understand many of the issues and opportunities facing organizations today.

FIGURE 1-4

Data on the move

The data from a single customer order is used in many business processes, contributes to many reports, and winds its way into many databases.

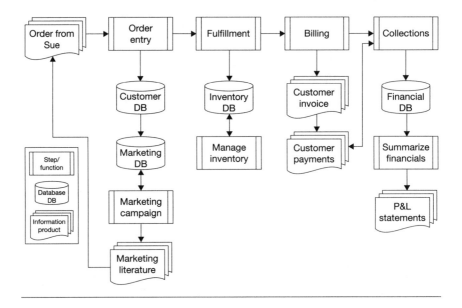

it. Sue could have saved five dollars had she ordered her granddaughter's sweater on the Internet. Still, she called customer service. Thus Sue's data contribute to Sweaters R Us's evaluation of its strategy.

Sue's order illustrates data on the move. I could have focused the example on Sue's data as they were stored in respective computer systems, such as the order entry system, the inventory management system, and the accounting system. But data in databases are less interesting. They don't help create any value sitting in a database. They can and do when they are on the move.

The upside is clear: even the simplest datum can contribute in many, many ways. The downside is also clear. First, bad data are like a virus. There is no way of telling where they will turn up or the harm they will cause. One woman recently told me that some of her personal data were entered incorrectly the day she was hired by a new company. She found out about it the next day, when setting up her e-mail account. In the course of correcting the original error, she found that nearly a dozen systems had been infected with the incorrect data!

The second issue is that it is hard to determine who "owns" or is responsible for data on the fly. One could argue that customer service owns the data because it created them. Or one could argue that order fulfillment, inventory management, or some other department owns the data because it needs them. Finally, one could argue that IT owns the data, because it manages the computers and systems that move the data around. There are obvious strengths and weaknesses to each candidate answer. Unfortunately, in too many organizations the question is simply left unasked.

There is only one possible course of action: organizations must get their arms around and manage their most important flows of data and information.

Data and Information Are Organic

As data and information zip around, they change and grow to meet the needs of the people, departments, and companies that use them. Order fulfillment, for example, focuses on getting Sue's package to her granddaughter, reliably and at low cost. It only cares what Sue paid for the sweater when the price crosses a certain threshold and it must insure the package. So for this department, data about price morph into a simple INSURANCE NEEDED flag.

Similar changes are needed in accounts payable, whose focus is on paying suppliers promptly and correctly. New data, keeping track of payments, are also created. Without belaboring the point, something similar happens in each department. As data move, they change and grow. Sue's original order provided two dates: the ORDER PLACED DATE and the PROMISED DELIVERY DATE. These morphed and led to SHIP DATE, SUPPLIER PAYMENT DATE, REVENUE RECOGNIZED DATE, and perhaps others.

Data and information seem to breed new uses for themselves. It is only natural that Sue's data are used to help answer basic marketing questions such as the following:

- "I've noticed a lot more male customers lately. Is that really true?"

- "We thought these new styles would have greatest appeal in hip cities like New York, London, Paris, and Tokyo. Do they?"

- "Are we getting as much repeat business as we hoped?"

Data as basic as street addresses, defined to support basic operations, are later used in marketing analyses that were simply not contemplated when the data were defined.

But there are limits to the versatility of the existing data. Sooner or later someone will ask, "We thought these new styles would appeal to those with the highest disposable income. Do they?" This question, and plenty like it, cannot be answered with the existing data. Sweaters R Us must expand its data model and adjust its business processes to obtain the newly required data. Thus the new data needed to support demographic analyses are born. Sequences like this play out all this time. Figure 1-5 sums up these points, illustrating the virtuous spiral between data and information.

As the examples illustrate, data lead interesting lives. But sooner or later, people and departments lose interest in Sue's data. Although they may be stored safely away on an optical disk array or some other medium, they have, for all practical purposes, been retired. They may be needed at some later date if there is a dispute, either with Sue, the delivery company, or the supplier. But the working lifetime of most data such as Sue's is very short (see "The Long Lifetimes of Data Models").

Like everything regarding data, there are important exceptions to this rule. Data analysts and miners use long histories of detailed data to develop better explanations of the past and make better forecasts. And data live on as contributors to financial reports and other summaries. Finally, of course, data that have been carefully stored can be resurrected if and when needed.

All this activity leads people to say that "data and information are organic."[7] It is not literally true, of course. Real organisms are born, grow, change, combine with other organisms to breed new organisms, and die on their own. Data aren't actually doing any of those things. People are doing them to the data, either directly or more often via their computer surrogates. The analogy is important and useful, however. It recognizes

FIGURE 1-5

The virtuous spiral between data and information

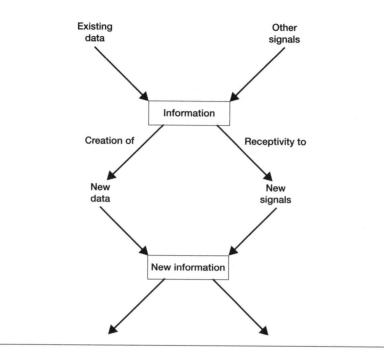

that data can change forms to suit the specific needs of different people and departments. It underlies the many ways in which it is possible to bring data and information to the marketplace. It is through their growth, changes, and combinations and recombinations that data add value. And, of course, all these changes are uniquely an organization's own.

The complexity can run amok, however. In most organizations, the events described earlier are mere happenstance or, worse, are addressed in a half-hearted fashion. For example, Sweaters R Us could have included demographic data in its initial systems design. So too data about whether customers intend to wear their new purchases at work, play, or for high fashion; lifestyle data; and on and on. The trap is to conclude "It might be useful, so let's include it." The new system then becomes too expensive and cumbersome and doesn't do anything well. Too much data are never used for anything. They are, in effect, stillborn.

The Long Lifetimes of Data Models

In contrast to individual data records, which usually have very short working lifetimes, the underlying data models often lead long lives, outlasting systems and entire generations of managers. This is because well-designed data models capture the underlying structure of the organization, which also changes slowly. Given this fact, managers would be well advised to invest the time and resources required for this oft-misunderstood effort.

Thus, managers must harness the data life cycle, from birth through growth and change all the way to retirement.

Data and Information Can Be Shared, Lost, or Stolen

To a greater degree than any other asset, data and information can be shared with others. Some historians opine that mankind's most important invention was the printing press because it made for faster and easier information sharing. Advances in communications and computer technologies continue the trend, making it easier to transmit data over long distances and at the speed of light. I have already noted the advantages that result. No other asset offers the potential to align the organization on common tasks or to be built into multiple products and services. This property has no counterpart in other assets.

Of course, the reality is much more complex. True sharing involves more than simply transmitting the data to the next person. You have to explain the subtleties in your data, their strengths and weaknesses, and other points that help the next person use your data effectively. This is at best a time-consuming task, with little chance of reciprocation. Further, some people intuitively realize that data are power in the Information Age, and they don't want to share. I'll expound at length on this topic in a later chapter.

Finally, I already noted that the fundamental property of data is not that they can be shared, but that they can be digitized, transported, and copied at very low cost. This presents complications because data are thus easy to steal. With most assets, you can tell whether someone has stolen them because they are missing. But data thieves don't actually have to go to the trouble of removing data—they simply transmit a copy to themselves.

Interestingly, it may seem that the ease with which data can be copied and transported presents a solution to the ownership question cited earlier. Why not let all departments—indeed, every individual—have their own copy? Intriguing, but then who is responsible for ensuring that all the copies are kept current when a new data value is created? Unless copies are synchronized, the multiple copies will soon be horribly misaligned. And who is going to keep track of and protect all those copies? Different questions, perhaps, but no less troubling.

Data and Information Are Not Consumed with Use

When an organization spends a dollar, it no longer has that dollar. When it sells a product item from inventory, it no longer has it. And when it assigns an employee to work on one project, his or her availability for other projects is reduced. Using most assets consumes them. Not so with data. Use them and you still have them. Send them to a customer or informationalize a product, and you still have them. You can use them over and over—they never wear out. Further, data can have incredibly long lifetimes. They outlast mergers, downsizings, new computer systems, even entire generations of managers.

Data miners appreciate this property. They love long historical records because they use the past to see cycles and project them forward. The longer the historical record, the more cycles they can identify. Nonconsumability can be a liability as well. It lies at the root of Stephen Brand's observation that "information wants to be free."[8] If you sell your hard-won data or information to someone, they can resell it—or give it away, which is an important consideration when one is trying to make a business selling data and information.

Long data lifetimes can be a liability as well. They mean that your secrets are never safe from the prying eyes of litigants and regulators.

Nonconsumability is a fascinating, as yet poorly understood property. It seems likely to me that we'll discover other potential benefits and liabilities of this property as the Information Age matures.

Data Are the Means by Which Organizations Encode Knowledge: They Are Meta-Assets

There is a popular model that I summarize as follows: "Knowledge is derived from information, which is in turn derived from data." Some go even further, pointing out that wisdom can be derived from knowledge. This is an important insight, and I explored half of the insight— how information is indeed derived from data—earlier in this chapter. I also pointed out that the process worked both ways, with information generating new data. The reverse process is no less true for knowledge.

Knowledge, by its very nature, is tacit and hard to pin down. It's in the heads of employees. If data are intangible, knowledge is positively ethereal, and it is difficult to share and leverage. The only solution is to carve out the portions of knowledge that can be more clearly defined as data and information. Not all knowledge can be so defined, and the process of encoding the less tacit portions can be tortuous. But, so far anyway, there is no other choice.

Furthermore, the day-in, day-out data are not just assets, they are *meta*-assets, the means by which organizations know about their other assets. Organizations have financial data, property data, and employee data, which are essential for managing these assets. When these data are missing, incomplete, inaccessible, inaccurate, or hard to understand, managing the other assets becomes that much more difficult.

Data and Information Are Intangible

Whereas one can see data records, data values themselves are intangible. This means they have no physical properties, such as the length of a manufactured product, the age of an employee, or the impedance of an electrical component. The good news is that you don't need much space to store them.

The downside is that it's harder to manage something you can't see or feel. Too often, data are "out of sight, out of mind" and therefore escape management attention. Perhaps that is one reason organizations have yet to fully recognize data and information as business assets. Further, because they have no physical properties, they are much harder to measure. There is no "accurometer" or other simple means to tell whether data are correct. And, as every manager knows, you can't manage what you can't measure. Chapter 3 discusses ways to finesse this issue.

Each Organization's Data and Information Are Uniquely Its Own

I began this chapter by asserting that an organization's data and information are uniquely its own. The high rates of data creation; the ways they create value as they move around, morphing to meet new needs as they go; the built-in nuance and close connection to business language; and the way they breed new uses for themselves all contribute to making this so. This point bears repeating. Each organization has, and always will have, the ability to think about customers in its own unique ways, to capture different data about customers, and to use those data differently to create its own niche. This point extends to all data. No other organization has, or can have, the same data about marketplaces, products and services, processes and operations, other assets such as people and plants, and so forth. Even better, an organization's collection of data grows richer each day and is not consumed when used.

Further, unlike a patent, the data never expire. And unlike employees, they cannot be hired away. Data and information don't even walk out the door at night (unless, as noted previously, you let the bad guys steal them). Because this will always be the case, data and information may well qualify as the "ultimate proprietary assets," there to be nurtured and expanded, looked at in new ways, and combined and recombined in the marketplace by this and future generations. The potential is limitless.

Reflecting on these points, Jeff McMillan of Merrill Lynch noted, "When you think about it for a minute it strikes you. Organizations are increasingly sophisticated at technology deployment, financial controls, and process management. The marginal returns from further investments are small. Investments in data are quite the opposite. The opportunities are limitless. And, more importantly, any investment you make is proprietary to your business. This is the true definition of competitive advantage."[9]

THE BIG PICTURE

- ➤ Your data and information assets are yours and yours alone. No other organization has your data or your capacity to make more.

- ➤ Shed any preconceived notions you may have about data and information. Ditch the impression, if you harbor it, that "Our most important data are stored on corporate databases and so are the province of the IT department" or the preconceived notion that "Clerks deal with data; I deal with ideas." Even if these notions are true, they are incomplete. And they are more likely misleading.

- ➤ Think of data and information not as the stuff stored away in the database, but as organisms that come into existence with surprising rapidity and cross organizational barriers in the blink of an eye, multiplying and morphing as they go. They can be digitized, transmitted, and copied endlessly, so they can be shared to an almost limitless degree. They are not consumed with use, so you and everyone in your organization can use them over and over again in new and creative ways, which in turn suggests new questions to be answered. These assets have wormed their way so completely into the organization's psyche that business discourse is not possible without them.

- ➤ Every possible benefit comes with a cost. Information technologies increase both the promise and the peril. Although getting the most out of data will involve computers, doing so is not, at its heart, a technological problem.

- ➤ Getting the most out of data and information is largely an issue of management and leadership. No technological wizardry can force one department to gather data it does not need for another, force people to adopt new language, or make people share data they really do not want to share.

➤ Data are more complex than they appear. Everyone touches data in some way or another, and getting the most from them will require the coordinated efforts of virtually everyone.

➤ Many desired behaviors, such as data sharing, do not come naturally. If leaders expect people and departments to behave differently, they will have to define and implement incentives and disincentives to encourage the behavior they seek.

➤ Some data may contain many secrets that can separate your company from others. Other data, perhaps most, contain no such secrets. But the data do not give up their secrets easily. Management must tease these secrets from them.

I

Data Quality

CHAPTER TWO

The (Often Hidden) Costs of Poor Data and Information

I find that most good managers today are well aware that their organizations suffer from bad data, but they don't know enough to properly slot data quality on their To Do lists. They may still view data quality as an arcane technical issue, albeit an annoying one—certainly not something that can land their companies in any real trouble. They don't yet see bad data lurking just beneath the surface as the root cause of or as an important contributor to their organization's most important challenges. Similarly, the accounting system doesn't have a category entitled "costs/risks due to bad data," so managers have no window into the cumulative impact of the problems that they do see.

This chapter seeks to bring poor data quality out into the open, using recent news accounts to help managers train themselves to see bad data and its impact. Indeed, bad data land organizations in deep trouble with disturbing regularity. The chapter then highlights the seven most common problems and provides benchmarks for each. Even if one can avoid deep trouble, the day-in, day-out costs of poor data are simply enormous (think 10 to 20 percent of revenue). Therefore this chapter also introduces the cost-of-poor-data-quality mosaic as a means to help managers smoke out these mostly hidden costs. Finally, and perhaps most importantly, the chapter aims to inspire managers to baseline data quality in their organizations.

"Where There's Data Smoke, There's Business Fire": The Subprime Mortgage Meltdown

The subprime mortgage meltdown began in 2007 and, at the time of this writing, is far from over. It illustrates perfectly how bad or missing data contribute to issues of international importance and the costs and uncertainties that result. Through the data and information lens, the subprime meltdown also perfectly illustrates that "where there's data smoke, there's business fire," the Information Age update of the familiar "where there's smoke there's fire."

The meltdown has its roots in two financial innovations that offered home ownership to millions of people who previously had not qualified:

- New mortgage products with low introductory rates (with lower initial payments, more people qualified)

- Collaterized debt obligations (CDOs), designed to package mortgages in ways that reduced and spread risk

Thus a mortgage originator could provide mortgages to subprime applicants and sell these mortgages to financial institutions. These financial institutions in turn packaged these mortgages with others into CDOs, with commensurate risk and return, and sold them to investors.

Bad data and information contributed to the debacle every step of the way. First, many mortgage applications included incorrect (possibly falsified) income and other data, thus allowing some unqualified applicants to obtain mortgages. Another contributing factor may well have been the decreased accuracy of credit scores for predicting the likelihood that a borrower would repay the debt.[1] Lenders, in other words, did not have the accurate data they needed to judge whether a mortgage should be granted. Conversely, many mortgagees appear not to have understood the terms of their mortgage. Most important, they did not understand that their interest rates, and hence their monthly payments, could go up significantly.

Second, CDOs are extremely complicated products, and many investors appear not to have understood what they bought. Purchasing securities is always complicated, and many investors turn to the ratings provided by independent agencies such as Moody's and Standard & Poor's. Indeed, some pension funds can only purchase securities rated "investment grade" by these agencies. Quite evidently, numerous ratings have proven incorrect. At least one ratings agency defends itself, claiming that it publishes "opinions" only, and that these opinions should not be trusted for investment decisions.[2] But it matters little to investors whether they were not informed on this point or the ratings they trusted were simply wrong.

As mortgagees have defaulted, those who thought they held the mortgages have started foreclosure proceedings. But in many cases, they have been unable to produce the paperwork that proves their rights, and judges have halted the proceedings.[3]

Finally, there's the credit crunch. A major contributor is that banks lack the data to properly determine which securities are at risk and value them accordingly. The only logical reaction is to lower credit limits, raise rates, and tighten lending requirements. Banks aren't even lending to each other, as they don't fully understand each other's liabilities, either.[4]

As of February 2008, the meltdown has already caused thousands to lose their homes, led numerous companies to file for bankruptcy, forced financial institutions to write down assets by over $150 billion, and claimed the jobs of two CEOs at major investment banks.[5] If that weren't bad enough, the uncertainties continue to loom large. As noted above, companies and policy makers are still unable to properly size the issues. Are further write-downs imminent? If so, how much will be involved? How many people will lose their homes or jobs? How broadly and deeply will the meltdown affect other parts of the economy? Unfortunately, no one knows. One well-known economist, Paul Krugman, goes further, arguing that the subprime crisis is more properly a "crisis of faith."[6] Financial markets depend on "trust," in security descriptions, in ratings, in balance sheets, indeed in the data that support any transaction. Once lost, it may take years to regain.[7]

Data quality issues are not confined to financial services—far from it. Practically everything in modern society depends on timely, well-defined, accurate, and trusted data. Unfortunately, "data quality disasters" litter the news. Almost every day, some newsworthy item has poor data quality at its root.[8] This is not the kind of exposure that organizations desire. No sector, no industry, no organization, no operation,

---

The Dirty Dozen

1. **Subprime mortgage meltdown:** This issue was discussed in detail earlier in the chapter.

2. **The 2000 presidential election:** Perhaps the most infamous data quality debacle in recent times occurred during the 2000 presidential election. The whole world watched with rapt attention as counties in Florida counted and recounted votes for candidates George W. Bush and Al Gore. Thirty-six days elapsed before Mr. Bush was declared the victor.[9]

   A Caltech–MIT team of computer scientists, mechanical engineers, and political scientists concluded that some four to six million votes were lost across the country during the 2000 election.[10] What happened in Florida could have happened anywhere. And it does, as the 2004 gubernatorial race in Washington State attests. Christine Gregoire lost by 261 votes to Dino Rossi in the original count and by 42 votes in an automatic recount, but won by 130 votes in a second (and final, under Washington law) recount.[11]

3. **Mars spacecraft:** A $125 million spacecraft was destroyed on a mission to Mars in 1999. The craft successfully navigated over 400 million miles, only to be destroyed because NASA failed to convert English units of measurement to metric units.[12]

4. **Fort Monmouth closing:** The 2005 Base Realignment and Closing Commission recommended that Fort Monmouth (in New Jersey)

---

no line of work, and no collection of data is immune to the ravages of bad data. See "The Dirty Dozen" for excellent examples of real-life data quality problems, illustrating that bad data can indeed land organizations in deep trouble. In reading through, try to spot the inaccuracies, poor definitions, and other data quality issues at the root of the problem.

---

be closed, in part based on incorrect data about the cost to move its function to another base, incensing businesspeople and politicians.[13]

5. **Trader assistant's error:** A computer error halted trading in Japan's municipal bond market for two hours in June, 2006, after a trader's assistant transposed two numbers: the number of shares to be sold (1) and the price (¥640,000). The data mix-up ended up costing his firm approximately $350 million.[14]

6. **Misgraded SATs:** About four thousand students who took the SAT in October of 2005 received inaccurate test scores because of technical problems in the scoring process.[15] Some students lowered their expectations and did not apply to schools on their initial lists. Others may have been denied admission to their first choice. Some students may have gotten into schools that are too tough. Overall, it is impossible to know the impact.

7. **Jésica Santillán and Kaiser Permanante:** Quality data are vitally important in health care, where people can die as the result of incorrect information. Seventeen-year-old transplant patient Jésica Santillán died after organs of the wrong blood type were used in her operation.[16] In a separate case, poor data quality at a Kaiser Permanante kidney transplant center caused deadly mismanagement of the donor waiting list.[17]

8. **Department of Veteran Affairs laptop:** A laptop computer containing personal data on over twenty-six million veterans was lost by an employee of the Department of Veteran Affairs. Although this episode ended happily when the laptop was recovered with all data

---

continued

intact, it rightly embarrassed officials. Other instances may not end so well: dozens of companies, managing the personal data of eighty-eight million people, have either lost customer data or had customer data stolen.[18] More recently, two CDs containing personal data on twenty-five million British citizens and seven million families were lost in the mail.[19]

9. **Law enforcement and 9/11:** The best-known example of law enforcement and intelligence communities failing to connect the dots occurred when data that might have prevented the terror attacks of 9/11 were not shared and properly analyzed. (Clearly, it is impossible to know for certain whether the attacks could have been prevented, but most experts agree that the data added up to warning signs that were ignored.)

10. **Financial reporting:** Led by the scandals at Enron and WorldCom, incorrect financial reporting dominated the news in late 2001 and 2002 and continues with disturbing regularity.[20] Even when there is no suggestion of wrongdoing, hundreds of financial statements have been restated because errors were found.[21] One impact is that many investors don't look at the subprime meltdown as an isolated case, but rather as part of a larger ongoing issue.

11. **The 2000 census:** Virtually everyone in the United States is affected when national census data are incorrect. Although the news accounts discuss the political reactions to statistical methods, the unpleasant fact remains that some people were not counted in the most recent census and others were counted twice.[22]

12. **Intelligence:** The CIA selected only one bombing target during the entire Kosovo war. But an incorrect map led it to pinpoint the Chinese embassy rather than the headquarters of the Yugoslav Federal Directorate for Supply and Procurement.[23] The suspected presence of weapons of mass destruction contributed mightily to the case for the Iraq war. A 2007 National Intelligence Estimate on nuclear weapons in Iran completely changes an earlier (2005) assessment, concluding that Iran terminated its nuclear weapons program in 2003.[24]

Seven Common Data Quality Issues

Most data quality issues don't make the front page. And a list of anecdotes, no matter how long and impressive, does not the general case make. Over the years, however, consulting shops, software providers, industry analysts, and practitioners have studied data and information quality more broadly. Their studies suggest that the published accounts are by no means unusual.

It bears repeating that bad data are an equal-opportunity peril that bedevils every organization—large or small, public or private, foreign or domestic. All data—customer data, product data, financial data, and employee data alike—are at risk. Bad data affect all departments—operations, sales, marketing, and finance. No one is immune. Table 2-1 provides a summary of seven common data quality issues and benchmarks for each.

TABLE 2-1

Seven common data quality issues and benchmarks for each

Issue	Benchmark
People can't find the data they need	Knowledge workers spend 30% of their time searching data they need, unsuccessfully half the time.
Incorrect data	10–25% of data record contains inaccuracies
Poor data definition	Data frequently misinterpreted
	Can't connect data from different departments
Data privacy/data security	All data subject to loss
	Risk of identity theft
Data inconsistency across sources	The norm when there are multiple databases
Too much data	Half of all data never used for anything
	Uncontrolled redundancy
Organizational confusion	Can't answer basic questions such as:
	1. How much created each day?
	2. Which are most important?

People Can't Find the Data They Need

Studies suggest that knowledge workers spend up to 30 percent of their time searching for the data they need.[25] Studies also reveal that searches are unsuccessful about 40 percent (when searching the corporate intranet) to 50 percent of the time or more (when searching the Internet).[26] An Accenture study yielded a slightly lower figure on search time and reported that half the information found was of no use.[27]

Incorrect Data

The easiest problem to understand is inaccuracy, where the data values disagree with their real-world counterparts. Although there is considerable variation from database to database and organization to organization, a good estimate is that 10 to 25 percent of data records contain errors (including data that are simply missing).[28] It is hard to imagine a more sobering statistic. It implies that 10 to 25 percent of hospital records contain an error. That 10 to 25 percent of telephone bills contain an error. That 10 to 25 percent of customer records contain an error. And, because even a routine decision requires many data records, virtually every decision must be made in the face of inaccurate data. Seen in this way, the stories making the newspaper are not so surprising.

Too Much Data

At the same time, organizations are buried in data they never use. In the Accenture survey, a full 40 percent of IT managers complained of information overload. Perhaps half or more data are never used by anyone for anything.[29] Of course, storing data is cheap. However, continuing to collect data that no one will ever use is not. It takes time and money and keeps people from focusing on more important data.

Overload comes in other forms as well. One organization privately reports that it has twenty-seven copies of one of its most important categories of data. Lots of fiefdoms wanted their own copy, and they got them (in answer to the reader's unvoiced question, yes, this organization is far too rich). Although twenty-seven copies is atypical (ten copies seems about average), most organizations have far too much data redundancy.

Data Inconsistency Across Sources

Redundancy contributes to another problem—inconsistency. Even two copies, once identical, can soon disagree, confusing knowledge workers and stifling the effort any time two departments need to work together. Perhaps anticipating the problem, Mark Twain observed, "A man with a watch knows what time it is. A man with two is never sure."

Poor Data Definition

Another critical data quality issue involves poor data definition. An example cited earlier involved confused units of measurement that caused a spacecraft to burn up. Like this example, most definitional issues are specific to the organizations that experience them. But some have broader impact. My favorite example involves the former planet Pluto. As every schoolchild knew, Pluto was the smallest and most distant planet. No more. With great debate and considerable disagreement, scientists have modified their definition and Pluto is now but a "dwarf planet."[30] Our children must thus learn a new mnemonic for the order of the planets. "My very energetic mother just sat upon nine porcupines" will no longer do.

In many situations, customers require that data definitions be commonly understood across the organization. Four records from various departments in a bank illustrate the point:

Passbook savings: John Doe Jr.

Mortgage: John and Mary Doe

Car loans: Mrs. M. Doe

Investment advice: Doe, J.

How many customers are there? How are they related? Are they from one household? How can you know?

Similar issues are the norm in all industries. A health care company needs a commonly understood definition of *treatment*, a logistics company of *address*, and a retailer of *household*. The lack of commonly understood definitions often masquerades under phrases such as "These systems don't talk to each other," "We can't develop a 360-degee view of our customers," or "You have to understand how things are done in legacy systems." But the real problem is the lack of clear, agreed-upon data definitions.

I don't have any hard statistics on the extent of this problem. Perhaps, as discussed in the next section, this is because the impact is difficult to quantify.

Data Privacy and Data Security

Privacy and security, or rather the lack thereof, are much in the spotlight right now. As the figures cited earlier confirm, identity theft is rampant. Over the past several years, a body of legislation has been enacted that requires companies to advise customers and employees when their personal data have been compromised. The news media seem keenly interested in the topic, so most egregious breaches are probably reported.

But if "people data" are not fully secure, then it follows that all other data are probably not as well. Hackers have been after data for years. In some cases, it is not even that difficult. For a time, critical information regarding base security could be purchased for the price of a used thumb drive outside U.S. Army bases in Afghani bazaars.[31]

Privacy violations can come in many forms. A company needs to know how old its employees are so it can plan for their retirements and make benefit decisions, but it cannot use age as a factor in a promotion decision. This example highlights an important point: some uses of data are simply not allowed. Keeping track is an onerous task.

Organizational Confusion

Although most organizations readily admit that data are critical assets, they cannot answer even the most basic questions concerning their data, including the following:

- What data do you have?

- Where are they?

- Which are the most important?

- How do you use them?

- Where do they come from?

- What are they worth?

Not having answers to these questions exacerbates the other issues. It is hard to see, for example, how an organization can protect personal data on a laptop if it does not know the data are there (see "Metadata Are Important Too"). Similarly, it is a waste of effort to improve the accuracy of data no one ever uses.

To summarize, too much data are just plain wrong, too hard to find, poorly defined, inconsistent with other data, and at risk of being lost or stolen. Organizations do not know what data they have, redundancy is out of control, and too much data are never used for anything. The last chapter pointed out that organizations create stunning quantities of new data. The net result is that they make more bad data every day.

Metadata Are Important Too

An important and often overlooked category of data is called *metadata* or sometimes *data resource data*. The fancy name aside, metadata are nothing more than data about data. All of the following, for example, are metadata:

- Data definitions
- Technical details of their physical storage
- Who may use them and permitted usages
- Who may not use them and prohibited usages
- Their original sources
- Systems that store them
- Details for gaining access
- Domains that the values may take
- Definitions of what those values may mean
- Conventions for naming the data and file structures

They are easy to overlook, but metadata are among the organization's most important data.

The Cost of Poor Data

Figure 2-1 shows the cost-of-poor-data-quality (COPDQ) mosaic, which is really nothing more than a way to keep track of the impacts caused by the problems cited in the previous section. This discussion will start on the top right, move counterclockwise, and hit some highlights.

It is easiest to see some of the ways in which poor-quality data increase cost in operations. As mentioned previously, knowledge workers spend 30 percent of their time searching for needed data—time that could be better spent analyzing the data.

Inaccurate data also add costs to operations. To illustrate, consider the process of completing a customer order. When all the data are correct, the transaction is completed quickly and at low cost. But, if any data are missing or incorrect—the customer's address is wrong, the

FIGURE 2-1

The cost-of-poor-data-quality (COPDQ) mosaic

The COPDQ mosaic lists costs and lost opportunities stemming from poor data.

inventory is incorrect, or so on—then the transaction takes longer and costs more. My *rule of ten* helps determine just how much more: *It costs ten times as much to complete a unit of work when the input data are defective (late, incorrect, missing, etc.) as it does when the input data are perfect.*

The rule of ten illustrates why even an apparently low error rate leads to enormous costs. For example, a 1 percent error rate may more than double the cost of a simple operation (see "Do the Math: Bad Data Are Extremely Costly"). A survey conducted by the Data Warehouse Institute included costs such as "lost mailings." It put the costs to American business at over $600 billion per year for *customer data alone.*[32]

Although the quantifiable costs are enormous, they almost certainly pale in comparison with the costs that cannot be quantified. My poster

---

Do the Math: Bad Data Are Extremely Costly

Many people are quite impressed with themselves when their data are "99 percent accurate." That sounds pretty good until one does the math.

Consider a simple operation, such as placing a customer's order that requires a dozen pieces of data. When the data are all perfect, the operation costs $1. Consider 100 orders. If all the data are perfect, the total cost is $100. One hundred orders each requiring 12 pieces of data means that 1,200 pieces of data are needed. An error rate of 1 percent means there are 12 errors. Chances are high that 11 or 12 of the 100 orders will be affected. The total costs are as follows:

Item	Unit Cost	Item Total
88 "good" orders	$1.00	$88.00
12 "bad orders"	$10.00	<u>$120.00</u>
	Grand Total	$208.00

The total cost has more than doubled!

---

child for this statement is the bombing of the Chinese embassy during the Kosovo war, cited earlier. The quantifiable cost is the $27 million the United States government paid the Chinese government. The real impact was that relations between the most populous, fastest-growing, and most powerful countries were set back two years—and it is impossible to calculate those costs.

Continuing around the COPDQ mosaic, the unquantifiable costs associated with customer dissatisfaction are especially important No one really knows, for example, the lost opportunity costs of angering a customer whose hotel reservation is lost. One study reports that 20 percent of people surveyed claim they will not do business again with a company that loses their personal data.[33] It is hard to translate that figure into hard dollars, however.

The impact of bad data extends far beyond operations. As I noted earlier, one of the ugliest meetings I ever witnessed involved a company that was evaluating the effectiveness of its recent marketing campaign. Two departments reported results as they saw them—one showed a "bump" in MARKET SHARE of a couple percent, the other nothing. Only after accusations were thrown and tempers flared did anyone notice that the two measures of MARKET SHARE were different. There was a perfectly logical explanation for the difference, but the damage had been done. It took months for people to simmer down.

Today companies are investing millions to implement the next generation of information technologies, replacing department-sized legacy systems with enterprise resource planning (ERP) systems, customer relationship management (CRM) systems, and data warehouses. Poor data are the number-one reason for the high failure rate of new computer systems. According to Ted Friedman of Gartner, "Through 2007, more than 50 percent of data warehouse projects will experience limited acceptance, if not outright failure, because they will not proactively address data quality issues (.08 probability)."[34] Tens of millions of dollars can be lost when these new systems must be scrapped or retrofitted.

Next, consider decisions at any level. It is trite to observe that decisions are no better than the data on which they are based, but veterans know the situation is far more lethal. When the data aren't trusted, sometimes an organization will study an issue ad nauseam, and no decision is made. Other times the result is even worse. A decision is made, but people are quick to point out its flaws. And they either don't align to accomplish the task or do so only half-heartedly. As all leaders know, you simply cannot execute a strategy without everyone's full support.

A special category of unquantifiable costs cuts across the COPDQ mosaic. I call it "the things that you simply cannot do because the data are too poor." When a CRM initiative fails, the organization incurs a high cost. It wasted a lot of money on people and technology. But a greater cost is that it simply cannot assemble a complete view of its customers, which means it cannot exploit opportunities to cross-sell, uncover new product niches, or craft strategies based on its most profitable customers. The true cost must also include all the revenue lost due to a failed customer strategy.

It bears repeating that poor-quality data affect strategy in a myriad of ways. They make it harder to select the best course of action, align the organization, and execute the plan. This point is especially applicable to all strategies for exploiting data and information. After all, there is no sense mining data if they are not accurate or you don't understand what they mean.

One final cost deserves mention. New laws and regulations related to data quality are continuously being promulgated and passed. The Sarbanes-Oxley Act, which placed new requirements on financial reporting, and the Health Insurance Portability and Accountability Act (HIPAA), for medical data, are probably the best known. Other laws and regulations mandate full disclosure of clinical trials, greater privacy, and increased transparency in executive pay. It seems almost certain that legislators and regulators will continue to ask for more and more. The long-term costs of compliance—and perhaps more important, noncompliance—are impossible to predict.

Finally, the wrapper around the COPDQ mosaic is "competitive positioning." Over the long term, it may be the most compelling reason to improve data quality. For, sooner or later, the quality revolution that began in Japan after World War II affects all industries. Actually, as Blan Godfrey, former head of the Juran Institute and now dean of the School of Textiles at North Carolina State, noted, the quality revolution isn't one, all-encompassing revolution. Rather, it is a sequence of mini-revolutions, each focused on a single industry. These mini-revolutions occur with stunning rapidity and reshape whole industries almost overnight.[35] Two industries bear special witness to this claim: consumer electronics and automobiles. By the mid-1980s, the Japanese had learned to manufacture superior color TVs, and a once-thriving industry left the United States. By the mid-1980s, the Japanese had also learned how to manufacture superior cars. U.S.-based companies fought off the challenge with a host of advances. But by the late 1990s they lost their focus on quality. Today, their very survival is in doubt.

Figure 2-2 summarizes the issues, representative statistics, and costs presented in the last two sections.

FIGURE 2-2

The current state of data in a typical organization and the immediate and long-term consequences

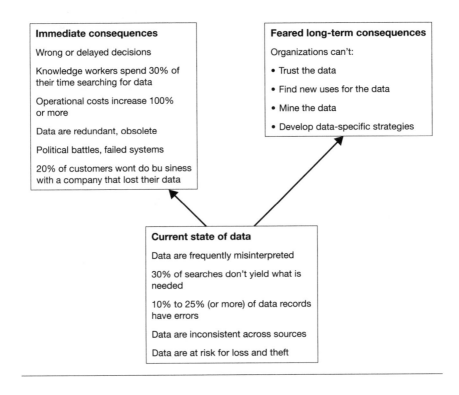

Immediate consequences

Wrong or delayed decisions

Knowledge workers spend 30% of their time searching for data

Operational costs increase 100% or more

Data are redundant, obsolete

Political battles, failed systems

20% of customers wont do bu siness with a company that lost their data

Feared long-term consequences

Organizations can't:

- Trust the data
- Find new uses for the data
- Mine the data
- Develop data-specific strategies

Current state of data

Data are frequently misinterpreted

30% of searches don't yield what is needed

10% to 25% (or more) of data records have errors

Data are inconsistent across sources

Data are at risk for loss and theft

THE BIG PICTURE

➤ Develop a keen eye for the roles data play in your job, including operations, decisions, connections between fouled-up operations, delayed decisions, and misinformed strategies.

➤ Select any initiative. Now ask these questions:

  – What data are most important to carry it out?

  – How good are those data? Accurate enough? Well-enough defined? How do we know?

  – How much easier would it be to carry out the initiative if all data were 100 percent correct?

  – What should we do about it?

CHAPTER THREE

Assessing and Improving
Data Quality

No one gets up in the morning and says, "I'm going to make lots of data errors today." Nor does any department head tell her people, "It's okay to make errors, just as long as we meet our quotas" or "I know you haven't been trained properly, but don't worry about the data. They're just for marketing anyway." The problems would be much easier to solve if they were founded in malfeasance. Or ineptitude. Or computer systems that weren't up to the task. I haven't found any of these to be the case. Instead, I find that a broad and complicated mix of social, cultural, and political issues conspires to make data quality such a tough issue.

This chapter is designed to help managers improve the quality of their organizations' most important data. It begins by describing how organizations with the best data approach data quality and the ten habits they apply to the task—how they think about the issue and what they do about it (see "How Those with the Best Data Do It").

Next, I'll describe some tools and role models that help managers assess their current data quality programs and get started. This is hard work. There is no silver bullet for data quality, nor is there a script for acquiring

---

How Those with the Best Data Do It

Approach: **How They Think About Quality**

Focus on *preventing* errors at their sources.

Ten Habits: **How They Do It**

1. Focus on the most important needs of the most important customers.

2. Apply relentless attention to process.

3. Manage all critical sources of data, including suppliers.

4. Measure quality at the source and in business terms.

5. Employ controls at all levels to halt simple errors and establish a basis for moving forward.

6. Develop a knack for continuous improvement.

7. Set and achieve aggressive targets for improvement.

8. Formalize management accountabilities for data.

9. Lead the effort using a broad, senior group.

10. Recognize that the hard data quality issues are soft, and actively manage the needed cultural changes.

---

the ten habits. Committed individuals start quality programs within their spans of control. They select the habits, often unconsciously, based on the problems and opportunities they face, their personal strengths and the strengths of their departments, their support (or lack of it) from above, their budgets, and the particulars of their situations. Some start with the more technical habits of measurement and control, deep in the bowels of operational departments. Others, marketers perhaps, struggling to understand what features should be included in the next-generation product, focus first on customers. Still others start at the top, with a focus on management accountability.

Tele-Tech Services, Interactive Data, and Morningstar started their quality programs using these three approaches, respectively. Each operates in a competitive "data market." Their data are put to the test every day. But their experiences are just as applicable to an organization's internal finance, market research, and operations departments, whose data never leave the organization. Their stories form the backbone of this chapter.

Approach Matters

Although there are hundreds of data and information quality tools and methods, all fall into one of two categories:

- Find and fix errors

- Prevent them at their sources

Most organizations pursue the first approach and get the results cited in chapter 2. Superior data requires a mind-set to prevent errors at the sources. It is the way the companies described here approach data and information quality. All ten habits assist in one way or other.

I often contrast the approaches using the so-called data quality lake. In this analogy, a lake represents a database and the water therein the data. The stream, which adds new water, is akin to a business process that creates new data and adds them to the database. The lake in the analogy is polluted, just as the data are dirty. Two factories pollute the lake. Likewise, flaws in the business process are creating errors.

In the analogy, one way to address the dirty lake water is to clean it up. You do so by running the water through filters, passing it through specially designed settling tanks, and using chemicals to kill bacteria and adjust pH. The alternative is to reduce the pollutant at the point source—the factories. The contrast between the two approaches is stark. In the first, the focus is on the lake; in the second, it is on the stream. So too with data. Finding and fixing errors focuses on the database and data that have already been created. Preventing errors focuses on the business processes and future data.

If preventing errors seems like the smart choice, it is. Departments and organizations find they can routinely eliminate 90 to 99 percent of errors this way and reduce costs, as dictated by the rule of ten, in doing so. Seen in this light, the business case is obvious.

Habit 1: Focus on the Most Important Needs of the Most Important Customers

Those with the best data adopt a customer-facing definition of quality. My favorite is based on the landmark work of Joseph Juran and reads: "Data and information are of high quality if they are fit for their uses (by customers) in operations, decision-making, and planning. They are fit for use when they are free of defects and possess the features needed to complete the operation, make the decision, or complete the plan."[1]

Who are these customers? Clearly, the organization's paying customers are data customers. Some companies sell their data, and even the most mundane products and services come with much data. A car buyer, for example, is a customer of the data that come with the car, including mileage estimates, financing details, and maintenance instructions. Other external stakeholders count as data customers as well. Shareholders and capital markets are customers of financial reports. Those with the best data even recognize regulators as customers (see "Regulators Are Customers Too"). Of course, most data never leave the organization. For these data, "customers" are internal and may be a person, group, or computer application. Finally, those with the best data may well recognize the organization itself as a customer. One example, as mentioned in chapter 2, is the organizational need to get everyone on the same page.

Those with the best data recognize that the needs of each customer may be quite different. Computer applications just do what they're told. The correctness of individual data values is of paramount importance, because incorrect data foul up transactions, increase costs, and anger customers. Similarly, data miners search for anomalies. They don't want to waste time tracking down "interesting data points" only to discover they are simply data errors. The accuracy of individual data values is less important when they are aggregated for use up the chain. Even a $50,000 error in an invoice, which infuriated a key customer and took weeks to reconcile, goes completely unnoticed when quarterly sales are added up. In contrast, both those up the chain and data miners place

---

Regulators Are Customers Too

He never said so directly, but I could tell that my father thought it was a bad career move when I went into quality. He had run clinical trials at Eli Lilly, the drug maker, and helped set up a subsidiary at HCA for the same purpose. We would talk about my work from time to time, and one day, after about five years of conversation, he called me up. "Tommy," he said, "I've finally figured out what this quality stuff is all about. It's about the 'customer.' All those years I spent at Lilly, we could never view the FDA as anything but the enemy. If we could have thought of them as the customer, we could have gotten drugs approved much faster."

I've told this story many times, in many industries. And the response is always, "You know, we should do that too."

---

high premiums on understanding what data mean, whereas computers could not care less.

The divergent needs of the three customers (the computer application, those up the chain, and data miners) illustrate a critical point: at any point in time, there are simply too many operations, customers to serve, and decision makers. Organizations cannot possibly meet all these customers' needs at once. Therefore, those with the best data focus on the "most important needs of their most important customers." This is a neat turn of phrase, but much harder to act on than to simply parrot. Three practices help:

- Connecting data and strategy

- Working through a hierarchy of needs

- Concentrating on leading-edge customers

In their landmark book *The Discipline of Market Leaders*, Treacy and Wiersema point out that excellent organizations don't try to be all things to all people.[2] Instead, they adopt and stick to one of a very few strategies. It follows that the most important data are those needed to execute that strategy:

- Organizations pursuing customer intimacy should focus first on deep, rich data about their customers.

- Organizations pursuing product leadership should focus first on the specific needs of leading-edge customers and on the details of product features.

- Organizations pursuing operational excellence should focus first on the data needed to keep costs low throughout the value chain.

Most customers and organizations exhibit a sort of hierarchy of data needs. My take on it is as follows:

The Data Doc's Hierachy of Data and Information Needs

1. *Acquisition:* A person or organization first seeks to obtain the data and information he, she, or it needs.

2. *Accuracy:* Once he, she, or it has the needed data, the next concern is that the data are correct.

3. *Understanding what they mean:* Once a person or an organization feels the data are "reasonably correct," the next concern is making sure that he, she, or it understands what they truly mean.

4. *Consistency across sources:* Once the data are understood, the next concern is understanding how the data fit with data from other sources. At this point, the organization or individual recognizes, implicitly at least, data as business assets.

5. *Privacy and security:* Once an organization realizes its data are business assets, its next concern is keeping them from others. Similarly, once an individual realizes that personal data are valuable, he or she becomes concerned about privacy.[3]

Simple as this hierarchy of customer needs is, it helps explain a number of things. First, it explains our intuitive feelings about data and information. You must have them before worrying too much about whether they are accurate, and you're reticent to use data you can't trust. You don't require a deep understanding of what they mean until you start to use them in new ways. Finally, you only have to know how they relate to other data when you wish to truly exploit them.

Second, it explains why organizations have, to date, focused so much attention on information technologies—they needed these technologies to acquire the data and get them to people. Although much work remains, beginning to meet this need has been the major achievement of phase 1 of the three-phase Information Age.

Finally, it explains why organizations have worried so little, perhaps wrongly, about security. To the thieves, gaining access is their first priority. The countermeasures required by organizations are the fifth step on their hierarchies, and companies have simply not worked their way through the first four. They do not yet fully appreciate data as business assets, and protecting data does not have the same priority as gaining access has to the thieves.

Organizations with the best data work their way through the hierarchy, evolving their quality programs as the needs of their most important customers evolve.

An important concept is the notion of a *leading-edge customer*. Some people or organizations just have more richly developed intuitions about the way industries and markets will evolve. They are especially good "most important customers." Having understood their point of view, one noodles through the data and quality levels needed to pursue that view. Leading-edge customers are especially helpful because they help the organization get in front of other, less forward-thinking, customers.

The needs of leading-edge customers played a key role in moving Interactive Data forward, as described in the following case study.[4] Whereas to Interactive Data a "customer" is indeed a paying customer outside the company, the case is just as relevant to a department whose only data customers are internal.

CASE STUDY:

Interactive Data Teams with Clients to Advance Its Quality Program

Interactive Data Corporation is a leading provider of financial market data, analytics, and related services to financial institutions, active traders, and individual investors. Its twenty-two hundred people are based throughout North America, Europe, Asia, and Australia, and its headquarters are in Bedford, Massachusetts.

The company's pricing and reference data business provides pricing, evaluations, and reference data for more than 3.5 million securities traded all around the world. Financial services firms depend on data from Interactive Data Pricing and Reference Data ("Interactive Data") in many ways. Firms use Interactive Data's data to populate their security master files, which are vast databases of securities that can be bought and sold and to support trading operations. For example, certain descriptive data must appear on trade confirmations to clients. Some clients also utilize Interactive Data's pricing data and evaluations to help value their portfolios.

Financial services companies can be demanding customers. Their need for speed, accuracy, and greater coverage has grown and will continue to grow into the foreseeable future. To continue to ensure that its offerings meet the needs of clients, Interactive Data has continuously advanced its quality programs over the years. As an example, Interactive Data initiated new programs starting in early 2002 that focused on timely delivery. "Assembling and delivering our services is technical and demanding," observed John King, chief operating officer. "As our clients' business environments became more complex, being late by even a few minutes caused them headaches. So we knew we had to deliver on time, every time."

King and his team focused on two things to start with: making delivery status very visible and identifying and eliminating delivery bottlenecks. A simple RYG chart (red for seriously late, yellow for tolerably late, and green for on time) adorns the front door to the operations center, keeping the urgency of this work front and center. Identifying bottlenecks proved a bit tougher. As King observed, "Every time a delivery is late, there is some explanation. And you can wind up chasing your tail. The trick is to see the patterns—and eliminate whole categories of late delivery all at once."

The next push came when an Interactive Data client documented its requirements for descriptive data for North American municipal bonds, one of Interactive Data's largest security classes. In fact, Interactive Data covers approximately 1.2 million active municipal issues.

These requirements opened new doors. "Without these requirements, we simply had no way of assessing what was most important to the client," observed Mike Hunziker, head of quality assurance. "We knew from questions coming into our help desk that our data wasn't always meeting client needs, but we didn't know what was most important. With the requirements we could dig in and get the hard facts. This input from clients proved to be an important complement to our ongoing efforts to improve quality. They showed us a lot of things we were already doing well and several we could improve on." Thus Interactive Data began the patient work of project-by-project improvement. Each improvement was small, but had enormous cumulative impact.

"Client involvement was critical at this stage," according to Ray D'Arcy, president of sales, marketing, and institutional business development. "Like any other good company, we try to focus our time and resources on projects that will bring greatest value to our clients." The best progress is made when clients are involved. D'Arcy, somewhat philosophically, explained, "In those areas where clients have been directly involved, we've made rapid progress. It is simply easier to maintain focus when major clients are working with you on the effort."

The marketplace is rewarding Interactive Data's efforts. Sales continue to grow and, as D'Arcy noted, "We're winning against some very tough competitors. But what's even more gratifying is that we're building more trusting, longer-lasting, and better relationships with some of the best companies in the world!"

Trusting relationships have led to an unanticipated benefit. More and more clients have begun to suggest ways to enhance the data, in effect seeding the innovation pipeline. For Interactive Data, client feedback has helped strengthen their extensive quality control and improvement programs, which are designed to further improve data quality.

Habit 2: Apply Relentless Attention to Process

It stands to reason that if an organization is going to prevent errors at their sources, then it must manage those sources, down to the steps where data are created and any step along the way at which they are transformed or manipulated. Ultimately, there are only two sources:

- Organizations make data inside, via their business processes.

- They acquire data from outside suppliers.

Habit 2 is directed at internal business processes. Although it may well be true that "today's managers are enamored of process," I find considerable confusion about the subject, including its importance for data and information.[5] This section therefore describes how those organizations with the best data think about and manage their data and information processes today. As organizations grow more facile with the concepts of processes, I believe process management will continue to evolve and penetrate organizations more completely. Appendix A presents a historical perspective and suggests directions that I think will prove most fruitful.

As used here, a *process* is "any sequence of work activities, characterized by common inputs and outputs and directed to a common goal.[6] Simple enough. But note that the term, in and of itself, applies equally as well to the simple task of making yourself a cup of coffee in the morning as it does to multiyear efforts to integrate departments after a multibillion dollar merger.

I call processes such as unloading shipments, putting items in their proper places, and updating a computer system to reflect that work *little-p processes*. Taking customer orders and invoicing customers are other examples. Indeed, most operational work can be thought of as little-p processes. *Little-p* is a relative term—little-p processes are usually work group-sized or smaller, a "unit of work" can be completed in a few hours or days, and the actual work is conducted within a single department. From a management perspective, there are few organizational interfaces or handoffs.

Little-p processes are almost always parts of larger ones. For a retailer, the most important process might involve deciding on styles, deciding what quantities to order and reorder, obtaining this merchandise, advertising it, running promotions, and taking customer orders, as well as the little-p process of unloading merchandise, including all the data and information created and used throughout. For a shipper, the most important process might start with a customer request and track the movement of a container from an originating loading dock onto a truck for transport to a port, where it is loaded onto a boat; to the next port, where it is taken off the boat and put on a rail car; and finally to the destination loading dock. For a hospital, the most important process might start when a patient checks in, moves to his or her room and then through a sequence of clinics, laboratories, and operating theaters, and conclude when all the bills are paid. Note that data and information trails follows the container and the patient. These trails are part and parcel of such *big-P processes.* Organizations, even massive ones, have no more than a dozen or so big-P processes. Middle-p processes occupy the middle ground.

Process management is so important for data and information because few errors affect the people who create them. Instead, they surface far downstream. The unloader who enters the wrong SKU when unloading a truck doesn't hurt himself or his work. The error may not surface until weeks later, when a salesclerk has to tell a customer, "The system says we have five, but I can't find them." Well-managed processes connect people such as the unloader and the clerk. They ensure that the unloader understands how his actions affect the salesclerk, who in turn understands how her actions affect the person who orders merchandise.

The bigger the P, the more people, and departments, are connected and the lower the likelihood of downstream error. At the same time, the bigger the P, the greater the difficulties. Overhead increases, and the politics of managing across departmental lines can be brutal. Finally, there may be diminishing returns. After all, once the unloader understands that inputting the correct SKU is critical to the salesclerk, there is little gain when he understands that it is also critical to inventory management.

Organizations with the best data have found ways to accommodate this tension. They call out their most important processes, identify where those processes begin and end, and name process managers or process management teams and task them to think end-to-end. Their process teams avoid the trap of delving into the details—that is the job of functional managers. Instead they search for the neglected (and occasionally broken) interfaces that lead to erroneous data. In effect they work, in a nonjudgmental fashion, to manage the white space in the organization chart.

I find that (with a few exceptions) even organizations with the best data find metadata (i.e., data about data, including data definitions, standards, and catalogs) a bit more problematic. One organization, for example, struggled for two years to hammer out an agreement on a common definition for "client," only to have the effort negated in a subsequent merger. That said, managing the creation, deployment, and upkeep of metadata as end-to-end processes results in better metadata. Chapter 8 and Appendix C return to the subject of metadata.

Habit 3: Manage All Critical Sources of Data, Including Suppliers

From the perspective of a piece of data that is merrily going its way, lighting down in this database and that, helping various people with various tasks, and then moving on to the next person, departmental and organizational lines are but a blur in one enormous process. But from a manager's perspective the organizational boundaries matter. Done well, process management can extend across departments to the organization's boundaries—but not beyond.

Yet data obtained from upstream suppliers are of growing importance. Some external data, such as billing data, are quite mundane but have immediate financial implications. Other data, such as the demographic, customer, market, and performance data provided by specialist firms, are essential for operations and marketing. The quality of these data is absolutely critical.

It turns out that, in most situations, managing the quality of supplied data is not as difficult as it might seem. The quality revolution in manufacturing provides a role model. Manufacturers learned early on that high-quality products depended on high-quality parts, tools, dies, chemicals, components, and so on. At the same time, the cost of these supplied parts made up a high fraction of the costs of their products. Manufacturers therefore learned how to work with suppliers of critical parts. They learned how to clearly specify their requirements and help suppliers come into conformance. They learned that whipsawing critical suppliers on the basis of price alone did not serve their interests.

Of course, manufacturers were not naive. They adopted *caveat emptor* (buyer beware) as their watchword, and therefore insisted that suppliers measure their own quality against the manufacturer's requirements. They audited measurements carefully and fully inspected their suppliers' manufacturing processes. Those that came up to speed were certified and rewarded with more business. Those that did not were replaced.

As more and more manufacturers took advantage of just-in-time techniques, the demands for high-quality parts, delivered directly to the assembly line, *without inspection*, only grew. The costs associated with inventory and inspection simply were not sustainable. Just-in-time manufacturing requires tight integration of supplier and manufacturer. Today the best manufacturers work hand in hand with their suppliers on product and process design.

All of this did not unfold overnight. It took time for both manufacturers and suppliers to get over their initial mistrust of one another. It still doesn't always work perfectly, but the improved quality and lowered cost (mostly attributable, I think, to the reduction in the costs of "scrap and rework") attest to the power of supplier management.[7]

Supplier management is proving just as effective for data. AT&T, for whom supplier management had always been critical for its manufacturing arm, was among the first to extend supplier management to data, soon after it divested itself of local telephone companies over twenty years ago. The data were "invoices for access," and the biggest suppliers were the now-divested local exchange carriers. AT&T's efforts saved all parties tens of millions of dollars.[8] Since then, data supplier management has also proven its mettle in the financial services and retail sectors.[9]

Interestingly, I often find that it is easier to manage across organizational lines (that is, outside the company) than across departmental lines, inside the company. Several factors contribute to this situation:

- Both parties quickly find they have much to gain by working together.

- They recognize the difficulties of working across organizational barriers and so are more patient with each other than they are with internal people.

- They are not competing for the same resources.

Whatever the reasons, I find that data supplier management is a great way to begin a data quality program.

The Customer–Supplier Model

The customer–supplier model, depicted in figure 3-1, links the habits of understanding customers and their needs, process management, and supplier management (habits 1 through 3). This model, the selection of a customer-centric definition of quality, and statistical control (discussed shortly) are the three most powerful weapons in the data quality arsenal. Yet the customer–supplier model appears so obvious, so simple, that many miss its significance. Thus, it is worth a few words.

The customer–supplier model features three entities: your process, your customers, and your suppliers. The model expresses the notion that your process receives data and other inputs from suppliers, processes them in some way, and passes them on to your customers. The main line of the customer–supplier model thus tracks data on the fly from one step or department to the next. It recognizes those who receive your process's outputs as "customers," and it calls those who provide needed inputs "suppliers." The figure makes clear that the quality of product, service, or data you provide your customers is determined, in part, by the quality of product, service, or data your suppliers provide you.

One reason the customer–supplier model is so powerful is that it adjusts to clarify the perspectives of others. Either your suppliers or customers may occupy the central role. When suppliers are center stage, it is clear that you are a "customer" (even if they don't recognize you as

---

FIGURE 3-1

The customer–supplier model

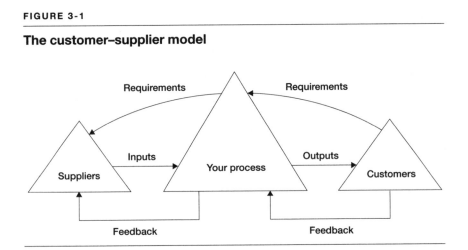

---

such) and that your suppliers have suppliers as well. When customers sit center stage, it becomes clear that your customers have customers too and that you are a supplier on whom they must depend to meet their customer needs. Figure 3-2 combines these points, fully illustrating the notion of data on the move. The figure could, of course, extend infinitely in either direction.

Note that "your process" in the center triangle of figure 3-1 can be replaced with "you personally," "your department," "your databases," "your business unit," or "your organization." Or it could mean "your decision," "your plan," or "your strategy." This is another reason that the customer–supplier model is so powerful—it scales down and up from actions as small as a role you might play for a few minutes in your organization to entire global companies, from little-p processes to the big-P processes.

Figure 3-2 also illustrates four communications (or back) channels for requirements and results. These channels are easy to miss, but they are essential—for "you" are extremely unlikely to meet your customer's needs if you don't know what they are. The requirements channel aims to ensure you do indeed know what is required (see "'They're Not Yelling at Me, So I Must Be Doing a Pretty Good Job'"). Just as important is the feedback channel, for "you" must know where you are meeting your customer's needs, where you are not, and the priority for improvements. Without feedback, "you" simply cannot improve. One can also think of the feedback channel as habit 4, measurement, linking the customer–supplier model to the technical habits.

FIGURE 3-2

Extending the customer–supplier model in both directions, illustrating the notion of data on the move

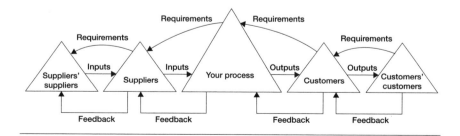

"They're Not Yelling at Me, So I Must Be Doing a Pretty Good Job"

As a consultant, the first questions I always ask are "Who are your customers?" "What are their needs?" "Are you meeting those needs?" and "How do you know?" I receive a range of answers, including quizzical looks, nasty stares, or a dissertation on how I don't understand their business (this last comment is frequently true). But I press on. One all-too-frequent response to all four questions is, "Those guys are tough. And I haven't spoken to them in over a year. But I know I'm doing a good job because they'd be yelling at me if I wasn't!" This response is a sure sign of trouble.

These same requirements and feedback channels are just as important between "you" and your suppliers. "You" simply cannot expect to get good data (or anything else for that matter) from your suppliers if you have not explained what you want and provided feedback. Suppliers are not mind readers. The Interactive Data case study is a perfect illustration of this point.

One thing that the customer–supplier model does not make explicit is who exactly is responsible for the communications channels. Is it "you" or those to your left and right? There is no simple answer. Most organizations acknowledge that they establish the communications channels with paying customers, but they feel no such need for non-paying customers or suppliers. "Why bother?" and "It's their job" is their reasoning regarding nonpaying customers and suppliers, respectively.

This reasoning is understandable, but those with the best data don't find it compelling. They know it is in their best interests to understand the requirements of their most important customers, whether they pay or not. Similarly, it is in their best interests that their most important suppliers understand their needs. If they have to make the first move, they do so.

Habit 4: Measure Quality at the Source and in Business Terms

Although subjective customer opinion is the ultimate arbiter of quality, objective measurements of process or supplier performance are essential, especially for data quality. This section focuses on accuracy.

Measurement is always problematic. Worse, data accuracy presents measurement complications unlike those encountered for any manufactured product. The most important stems from the fact that a datum is intangible. It has no physical properties, so there is nothing like length, weight, or voltage to measure. You can't measure it with a yardstick, scale, or voltmeter. A true "accurometer" simply cannot exist![10]

Fortunately, over the years, the scientific, statistical, and engineering communities have developed a sophisticated body of theory and practice, collectively known as *metrology*, for physical measurement. Likewise, data quality practitioners have developed a number of ways to get around the intangibility problem, at least to some degree, and there are now literally hundreds of choices. Picking the best one for specific circumstances involves four specific decisions:

- Where to take the measurement

- What measurement device to use

- Which data to include

- The "scale" for reporting results[11]

Those with the best data consistently opt for making measurements as close to the points of data creation as possible. Wherever possible, they compare data values to the real world. Doing so is expensive, so they employ small samples, but they measure continuously. They focus on the data elements most important to their customers. They report accuracy at the record level, because it better reflects business impact (see "Measurement Scales"). And they employ simple graphics such as the time-series plot of figure 3-3 to help them understand results.

Measurement Scales

The box in chapter 2 that illustrated the rule of ten gave an example featuring one hundred records of twelve fields each and a total of twelve erroneous fields, each in a different data record. The two possible methods of reporting accuracy yield the following:

$$\text{field-level accuracy} = 1 - \frac{\text{number of erred fields}}{\text{number of fields}}$$

$$= 1 - \frac{12}{1200} = 99\%$$

$$\text{record-level accuracy} = 1 - \frac{\text{number of erred records}}{\text{number of records}}$$

$$= 1 - \frac{12}{100} = 88\%$$

As that box explained, even one error can foul up the downstream business operation. In total, errors affect 12 percent of the work. The record-level measurement reflects this, whereas the field-level measurement hides it. The record-level measurement looks worse, but is superior!

Habit 5: Employ Controls at All Levels to Halt Simple Errors and Establish a Basis for Moving Forward

Organizations with the best data are facile with control, an oft-feared and misunderstood concept. Technically, *control* is the management action of comparing actual performance to standards and taking action on the difference.[12] A thermostat is a simple control mechanism. A person (the manager) chooses a desired temperature, and a thermometer measures the actual temperature continuously. When the actual temperature drops too far below the desired temperature, a signal is sent, turning on the furnace. When the temperature rises far enough, another signal is sent, turning the furnace off.

FIGURE 3-3

A typical time-series plot of record-level accuracy

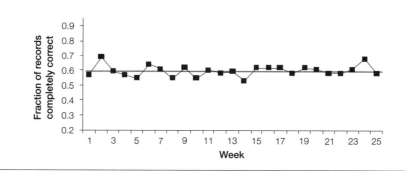

In the business world, everyone's least favorite control involves the budget. If your department is spending too much money, you will almost certainly receive a warning to cease—or else.

For data, there are two main types of controls. *Edit controls* comb through data records to identify anomalies, that is, records that do not look right (more correctly, data records that fail business rules). A simple example is as follows:

Title = Mrs., Sex = M

A data record featuring two such fields cannot be correct. Thus, the edit routine flags the field for further examination and correction.

Data edits can be quite sophisticated. Applied at the points of data creation, they are very effective. Most readers have probably noticed data edits in operation on good Web sites. These data entry routines make it more difficult for users to skip required data, enter nonexistent states or incorrect addresses, and so forth.

Statistical controls are even more effective (see "Statistical Process Control"). In figure 3-4, control limits have been added to the time-series plot of figure 3-3. These limits were derived from the week-to-week variation. In effect, they represent the process "talking" to management, communicating things such as the following:

- "Something unusual happened last week. You need to take a deeper look."

Statistical Process Control

I f you can put only one technical tool in your data quality quiver, make it statistical process control. The technique was invented by Walter A. Shewhart in the 1920s to help improve manufacturing in Western Electric factories. Winston Churchill once credited statistical control with helping American manufacturing produce the war materiel that overwhelmed Germany. It has had a storied history in industry after industry, and it is proving just as effective for data.

Mathematicians sometimes note the unreasonable effectiveness of their craft at explaining the real world. Statistical control is an excellent example.

- "I'm only capable of performing at 60 percent, plus or minus 15 percent."

- "It looks like those changes you made last month are really working."

Management must, of course, respond to the signals. One company that did just that is Tele-Tech Services, whose story is told in the following case study.[13]

CASE STUDY:

Statistical Control Propels Tele-Tech

Tele-Tech Services, based in Charleston, South Carolina, provides tariff data to the telecoms. Specifically, it performs the detailed technical work of translating the arcane legal terms of the thousands of tariffs filed in all local, state, and national jurisdictions into data that its customers can use to bill their customers. Family run and focused, Tele-Tech is the very model of an Information Age company: its employees are highly skilled, its customers depend on the data it provides, and, although it requires a sophisticated technological infrastructure, it is not a technology company.

FIGURE 3-4

Time-series plot with control limits

Here, an upper control limit (UCL) and a lower control limit (LCL) have been added to the plot of figure 3-3. Note that the process went out of control in week 26. It took several weeks to reestablish control.

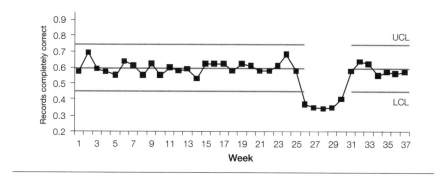

Like most niche data providers, Tele-Tech has always prided itself on quality. One of its founders, Steve Kromer, had been a long-time AT&T employee and was well versed in the mysteries of measurement, statistics, and quality improvement teams. Tele-Tech knew its quality approached 99 percent, and surveys confirmed that customers were quite pleased with Tele-Tech's services.

Still, Kim Russo, head of marketing, thought Tele-Tech could enhance its reputation by providing service-level agreements. Not only would the guarantee of "money back if we don't deliver" help customers feel confident, but also it would further distinguish Tele-Tech from its competitors. Russo's enthusiasm aside, the management team was skeptical. As Kromer remarked, "We were afraid that we would expose ourselves to all kinds of different measures that we might not pass. And we're just not rich enough to give back a lot of hard-earned revenue."

Tele-Tech dug in and took a hard look at what its customers really wanted and at its measurements. It found two things: first, although average quality was indeed 99 percent, the month-to-month variation was enormous. In the lingo of this chapter, accuracy was out of control. Second, large telecoms really did not want money back. Some were not even sure they could process a

Tele-Tech check. Instead, they wanted the data to be right—the first time, every time.

Stephanie Fetchen, head of technology and production, headed up efforts to establish control. "What we found was that we were quite good most months. But the months we weren't good, we were really bad. When we made errors, we made them in bunches." Everyone at Tele-Tech pitched in to complete a root cause analysis. They found a number of issues, mostly simple, that they were able to rectify. It has now been a year and a half since the last bad month. Errors still crop up, but one or two at a time. And the overall error rate is approaching one in ten thousand.

Tele-Tech has gone even further. It publishes quality reports every month. Customers see exactly what they get, as do competitors. And Tele-Tech has publicly committed to halving its error rate every year. There is no mistake whether or not it is on track!

Once it had its house in order, Tele-Tech expanded quickly to include first its customers and then its supplier base. The work with customers is beginning to bear fruit. As the telecom industry consolidates, Tele-Tech finds itself with a smaller and smaller base of potential customers. Thus, a successful future depends on innovation. Russo further noted, "Our best customers are proving to be great sources of new product ideas. They are suggesting all sorts of ways we can make our products more useful. Many go well beyond the conventional uses of our data for billing purposes."

Tele-Tech is well on its way to fully incorporating quality as its dominant management philosophy.

Habit 6: Develop a Knack for Continuous Improvement

Perhaps the best-known quality mantra is "continuous improvement." It embodies a spirit that recognizes that no matter how good any product, service, or collection of data is at any point in time, there is room for improvement. Two kinds of improvements are possible: adding features and eliminating defects.

Eliminating defects usually garners the most attention. There are dozens, perhaps hundreds, of good methods for finding and eliminating the root cause of defects. The best known is probably the Six Sigma DMAIC (*define, measure, analyze, improve,* and *control*) technique.[14]

Organizations with the best data have a knack for completing improvement projects. This statement is a lot deeper than it appears. Anyone can start an improvement project—the trick is finishing it. High-quality organizations are good at breaking enormous problems down into smaller, more doable ones and at assembling focused teams to tackle them. These organizations follow their improvement methodologies with rigor. They are especially good at making sure that once an issue is resolved, it does not recur.

These organizations extend the graph presented in figure 3-4 to look like figure 3-5.

Habit 7: Set and Achieve Aggressive Targets for Improvement

Quality improvement is not a haphazard occurrence in those organizations with the best data. It is purposeful and directed. Quality is front and center in planning activities. These organizations have learned to

FIGURE 3-5

Time-series plot showing improvement

An improvement project is completed in week 37, and control is reestablished by about week 45.

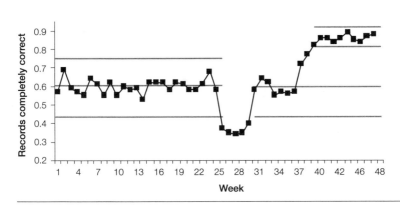

set targets for improvement that appear just out of reach and challenge their people to meet them.

A bit more subtly, perhaps, some organizations have learned to focus not so much on an actual quality level but on their rate of improvement. Targets such as "halve the error rate every year," the Tele-Tech target, or "add two new significant features every year" are really no different from targets such as "increase revenue by 8 percent" or "make two significant acquisitions."

There are many reasons that such targets are more effective than "achieve a quality level of 99 percent." Early on, an error rate of 30 percent to 50 percent (measured at the record level, according to the discussion above) can be very discouraging. Even after two rounds of improvement, the error rate may still be about 10 percent, which can be even more discouraging. It simply feels better to note that "we eliminated three of four errors last year and we're going to eliminate another three of four next year." Once quality improves to high levels, improvement targets keep the organization and individuals from resting on their laurels. After all, there is still more room for improvement!

Figure 3-6 adds targets for improvement to figure 3-5. Note how the sequence of figures 3-3 through 3-6 illustrates how habits 4 to 7—

FIGURE 3-6

Time-series plot with target

On seeing great progress, management sets an aggressive target for further improvement.

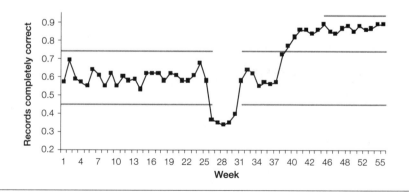

measurement, control, improvement, and aggressive targets—build directly on and reinforce one another. Collectively, they represent the technical core of data quality management and improvement.

Habit 8: Formalize Management Accountabilities for Data

Data quality programs tend to grow organically within organizations. Habits 1 to 7 are most often brought into the organization by a middle manager who uses them to address a specific problem. Gradually the habits may percolate down, across, and up the organization. If and when senior management sees the link between quality and performance, these habits spread rapidly.[15] In a relatively short period of time—say, five years for a large organization—they become the norm. This pattern was repeated again and again as quality revolutions took root in manufacturing industries.

The eighth habit involves clear accountability for data. The unspoken conclusion to the old adage "That which doesn't get measured doesn't get managed" is "That which doesn't get managed doesn't get done"—at least well and consistently. Heretofore, most organizations have not thought much about who specifically manages their data and information.[16] Some have concluded that their data and information were an appendage of the IT department. In fact, so many organizations have fallen into the trap of assuming that "our most important data are in the computer, so they must be IT's responsibility" that chapter 7 calls out the issue for special attention. From the early days of computerization, IT departments needed data management groups to define data structures, develop data dictionaries, and tune databases to optimize performance. One could conclude that they are the logical place for data quality, but so far they have not proven equal to the task.

Those with the best data recognize that data are more complex and so require a more sophisticated management approach. They understand that the management accountability for data must lie at the points of their creation, that is, with the processes of habit 2 and the suppliers of habit 3. Although responsibilities for data are thus highly diverse, they are also quite specific. The lion's share of work is in line, not staff, functions.

Many manufacturers have developed quality policies to document "who is responsible for what." The few that have extended these policies to data report good success.

Habit 9: Lead the Effort Using a Broad, Senior Group

Perhaps more than anything else, the seniority, breadth, and commitment of those leading the effort dictate how far an organization's quality program will go. A department leader can influence his entire department, and a business unit head her entire business. But to completely permeate an organization, its most senior leaders must be wholly committed. Joseph Juran, reflecting on the roles of senior management in manufacturing, stated it best when he said, "They thought they could make the right speeches, establish broad goals, and leave everything else to subordinates . . . They didn't realize that fixing quality meant fixing whole companies, a task that can't be delegated."[17]

Leading an organization's data quality program may be even more difficult, because data present perils simply not encountered in manufacturing. As we saw, virtually everyone touches data in one way or another and therefore can damage their quality. Data fly from one department to the next, virtually unseen. As noted previously, they are more difficult to measure because they are intangible. They are also more difficult to pin down.

It is not reasonable to expect high quality without broad, committed, senior leadership. Morningstar's leadership is a perfect example, as described in the following case study.[18]

CASE STUDY:

Leadership Drives Quality at Morningstar

Morningstar was founded in 1984 in Joe Mansueto's Chicago apartment. The mutual fund industry was experiencing dramatic growth, and it was extremely difficult for individual investors to learn about fund performance. Mansueto created Morningstar to fill that niche.

Morningstar has grown along with the financial services industry and technology innovations. Today it provides independent data and information on equities, variable annuities, closed-end funds, hedge funds, exchange traded funds, separate accounts, and 529 college savings plans, in addition to mutual funds. It continues to serve individual investors and also counts financial advisers and institutions among its customers.

Morningstar has always valued accuracy. After all, individual investors depend on its research and data to protect their retirements, grow their nest eggs, and fund their children's educations. So when it decided to formalize and expand its quality program in early 2004, the motivation was simple. Morningstar wanted to maintain and enhance its reputation for quality data in the face of the expanding range and number of instruments it covered.

Liz Kirscher, president of Morningstar's data services business, was selected to run the effort, an interesting and important selection for two reasons. First, Morningstar chose to locate its quality program within a business unit. Second, it placed such great emphasis on the effort that it chose that unit's president to lead the effort. As Tao Huang, chief operating officer, explained, "We didn't want a large bureaucratic effort. Instead we wanted something directly aimed at helping the business improve."

Kirscher embarked on a broad-based program. Accuracy, customer satisfaction metrics, and tighter internal controls topped her list. She also began experimenting with end-to-end process management on two important processes. With the basic facts and a management structure in place, improvement projects came next. Kirscher hired John Rong, a seasoned quality professional with experience at GE and Toyota, to help Morningstar understand process improvement. The first improvement projects took some time. Toward the end of 2005, however, the first wave was complete. Although Kirscher was pleased with the results, she was initially dismayed by the demands that introducing Six Sigma quality placed on her time. "I spend hours in reviews, getting involved in the deepest details of our processes," she commented. "Being able to see the improvement—through the measurement system we built—made people more open to reworking many of our long-standing processes. And we are pretty excited about our progress."

Next up for Kirscher and Rong is expanding the program. "We've had a great deal of success with our data quality, and we think process improvement can have a much broader application. We want to apply it to other, very different, areas of the business like client service and relationship management," Kirscher remarked.

Morningstar's revenue continues to grow, in no small part due to quality. Mansueto noted, "Quality is the top requirement for most of our clients and prospects. And there is a direct connection between our quality program and revenue. It [quality] wins us business in several ways. The measurements enable us to demonstrate that our processes consistently work well. People know they can trust us, and that has won us business. And we win business when prospects compare our data to our competitors' data. We win, hands down."

Habit 10: Recognize That the Hard Data Quality Issues Are Soft, and Actively Manage the Needed Cultural Changes

The last, but probably most difficult, habit involves the soft side of quality management, variously known as *people, politics, culture,* and *organization.* Chapter 7 discusses twelve specific social issues in depth, but of course there are hundreds of possible issues, and the ways in which they combine and interact are unique to each individual and organization. Quality is no different from any change in this respect: the tough parts of a merger or of the introduction of a new computer system or compensation system are also the social issues.

Unfortunately, there is no road map for addressing the soft issues. Organizations with the best data don't run away from the soft issues. They muddle along, working to understand the issues, acknowledging that reasonable people can see an issue differently, and seeking common ground. Like any other issue, acknowledging a problem is a necessary first step to solving it. I find that organizations with the best data tend to seek solutions that build on their strengths, not solutions that require them to first shore up their weaknesses. This point is important, because all have strengths—perhaps a long history of treating customers well, the depth of experience of the staff, a knack for working across departmental boundaries, or fresh young blood that has little invested in the past. Whatever these strengths, people and organizations simply seem

A Simple Model for Culture Change

In my consulting practice I use a simple model to help clients more actively lead cultural change. The model posits that four elements must *simultaneously* be in place if a change initiative is to succeed. I simply ask my clients to rate themselves on each element and work with them to improve the weakest link. The four elements are as follows:

- *Sense of urgency:* Essentially you have to answer the question, "Why is this deserving of my time and attention, given I'm already working too hard?"

- *Clear, shared vision:* You have to answer the question, "If I make the change, what is the new world going to look like?"

- *Actionable first step:* You have to answer the question, "So what do you want me to do differently tomorrow at 8 a.m., after I get my coffee?"

- *Capacity to change:* You have to provide time, training, money, anything else people need so they can actually contribute.

to move faster when building on their strengths rather than confronting their weaknesses. Finally, these organizations actively manage change (see "A Simple Model for Culture Change"). A cadre of business school professors had the insight, some years ago, that change is a process and that, like any other process, it can be managed.

If all this seems to be pointing to some sort of twelve-step program, it is. There are plenty of good descriptions of and tools for change management. Organizations with the best data pick one and apply it diligently.[19]

Assessing Your Organization's Data Quality Program

In reading through the habits, the reader may have kept score mentally, making comments such as the following:

- "No, that's not the way we approach data quality."

- "I guess customer data are most important."

- "The only thing we ever do with our suppliers is complain."

- "I'm sure we don't measure data quality."

- "The most senior guy who even thinks about data is some low-level guy in IT."

With mental notes like these, the reader may well conclude that his or her department is in deep trouble.

Maturity models are a popular means to baseline an organization's status as the first step in building needed capabilities for the long term. Figure 3-7 depicts the maturity model for data and information quality.

I call the lowest level *data unconsciousness*. Organizations at this level actually spend the most time on data and information quality, even though they don't know it. They bear the full brunt of the costs and risks

FIGURE 3-7

The data quality maturity model

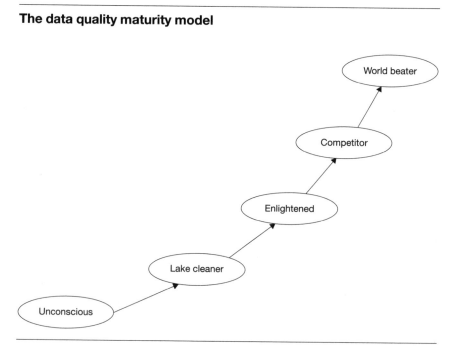

outlined in chapter 2. They are constantly bitten—employees are angry because they can't find the data they need, customer service representatives spend considerable time fixing errors for frustrated customers, and a third or more of the cost of a new technology project is spent in data issues. Many individuals in such organizations may be well aware of the poor state of data quality. The organization as a whole, however, doesn't see the patterns and is blissfully unaware of the high costs it pays.

In organizations at the next level, *data lake cleaners*, some people are hard at work on data quality issues within their workgroups. They've begun to implement better solutions within their spans of control. Perhaps they've figured out ways to address customer complaints more rapidly, perhaps they've added a step to check work before it leaves the workgroup, or perhaps they've added a number of computerized data edits to speed up error checking before issuing the monthly report. These workgroups address quality issues "in the lake," and they get lots of practice. Fortunately, because of individual initiatives, they are pretty good at doing so. Unfortunately, at the organizational level, these efforts don't add up to much. Individually good efforts amount to an unsystematic, uncoordinated, and unsophisticated attack on an enormous issue.

Organizations at the third level are more sophisticated. They have a comprehensive program for finding and fixing errors across the organization (i.e., they clean all the important lakes in a reasonably well-coordinated and effective manner) and they've made some real gains. There are still plenty of errors, but relatively few leak through to important customers. In essence, the good lake-cleaning efforts of level 2 pervade the organization.

The problem with being a good data lake cleaner is that life never gets better. Indeed, it gets worse as more data, more customers, and more demands conspire to mean there is more work every day. What really distinguishes a level 3 organization is that a few influential leaders (at any level) have grown tired of this work and refocused their efforts on preventing errors. They spend less time working in the database lake and more time working in the data streams feeding it. Consciously or not, they have implemented a quality habit or two. And, critically, they have experienced a solid success or two. They've had a taste and are eager for more. The rest of the organization may not care, or even know about, these successes. Those who have had a taste are not fated to see what they've experienced permeate the entire organization, but they are passionate to try. I call level 3 organizations *data enlightened*.

Readers used to seeing maturity models portrayed as a straight line, with each stage building on the previous ones, will notice a curve in figure 3-7 beginning in level 3. This curve illustrates that what elevates level 3 organizations above level 2 organizations is not that they do more level 2 activities better. Level 4 organizations are fully on the new path. It's not just a few committed leaders who have adopted the new thinking and several of the ten habits. There may be a central group leading the effort, and most departments are engaged. The organization is able to tackle larger issues, those that require a degree of cross-unit cooperation, such as developing a common definition of *customer* (an unconscious organization would not think to take up such an issue, and I would not recommend that a data lake cleaner do so). I call organizations at this level *data competitors*, because those who sell their data in the marketplace are formidable competitors. Of course, most data are not for sale. Equivalently, therefore, organizations at this level can trust their data in decisions, analytics, and other ways that emulate the rigors of the marketplace.

I call the fifth—and top—level *data world beaters*. They, and their customers, both internal and external, enjoy world-class data. From 2002 to 2005, a team led by Peter Aiken at Virginia Commonwealth conducted a survey of the data management practices of 175 organizations.[20] Although his survey questions and analyses don't quite line up with the criteria discussed here, he and I reexamined the raw data (and supplemented these data with personal experience to help correct for differences in focus) to conclude that the most common level (say, 50 percent of organizations) is level 2, the data lake cleaners. About 40 percent of organizations are at level 1, data unconsciousness, and 8 percent are at level 3, data enlightenment.[21] As of the time of the survey, only 2 percent had reached levels 4 and 5, data competitors and world beaters.

Evolving the Data Quality Program

All organizations starting a quality effort focus on two or three habits. They must—ten good habits are simply too many to acquire all at once.

But they don't stop there because, in the long haul, a few habits will not do. We all know of companies whose products are technically excellent but don't meet customer needs, companies that are very good at listening to customers but can't deliver, and companies whose management can articulate lofty goals that the rest of the organization does not support. All three case studies in this chapter reinforce the need for management direction, customer focus, and technical work to converge. Interactive Data's external focus is becoming the building block for internal work, Tele-Tech's technical excellence enables it to work more confidently with customers and suppliers, and Morningstar's top-down program is winding its way through the organization. Thus, the emphasis in organizations with the best data is less on the ten habits than on how they work together and fit into and help the organization's other management systems evolve. We've already seen how the customer–supplier model binds the managerial habits and how the technical habits build on each other. Those with the best data also work to build quality into everyday work. For employees in such companies, quality is not something they work on two hours a week. It is part and parcel of their everyday work.

THE BIG PICTURE

➤ Find and fix errors in existing data and information where you must. But recognize it as non-value-added work and get in the habit of eliminating errors at their sources.

➤ To start a data quality program, select the habits here that best help you get traction on a near-term business problem and opportunity. Understanding customer needs for a new offering, supplier management, and measurement are often good choices.

➤ Over time, add new habits to build an interlocking web of good data quality habits.

➤ Invest in building requirements and feedback channels with your most important customers and suppliers. The result is almost always significant, relatively easily attained improvements—and the improved relationships pay dividends for years.

➤ Define and name your most important big-P processes, even if you're not quite ready to take them on. The bigger and broader, the better.

➤ Don't expect miracles. Quality programs extend to the limits of their leaders' spans of influence.

➤ The hard issues are soft. Attend to them.

II

Putting Data and Information to Work

CHAPTER FOUR

Making Better Decisions

My second prescription calls for organizations to put their data and information to work both inside the organization and out. Inside, they must leverage them to speed supply chains, connect departments, develop a total view of the customer and understand customer profitability, first improve and then optimize their business processes, better manage their increasingly multinational employee base, ferret out unnecessary expense, and speed innovation. Indeed, they must make every employee a knowledge worker, driving data and information into every nook and cranny of every operation, customer interaction, decision, and plan. The focus of this chapter is doing so in decision making, because once decision makers get a taste for data and information, they will salivate at the chance to leverage them on the opportunities just noted, and ten thousand others as well.

Perhaps no management topic garners more study than decision making. After all, good decisions lead to better products, more revenue, increased market share, satisfied employees, and improved competitive position. They lead to promotions, big raises, and more responsibility. Conversely, bad decisions mean products stagnate, revenue falls, market share is lost, people become unhappy, and competitiveness is reduced.

It goes without saying that bad decisions wreck or, at best, stymie careers. Thus, there is much at stake.

There are a virtually limitless number of angles from which to study decision making, and many provide excellent insights for both managers and organizations.[1] But most, in my view, do not fully appreciate the roles data and information play and especially the debilitating effects of "facts" that are simply wrong. Nor do they provide insights into developing trusted sources in advance or systematically improving decision-making processes.

Make no mistake, the surest way to make and execute better decisions is to fully leverage data and information:

- By having better data and information in advance

- By using them to make better, faster decisions

- By using them to align the entire organization and thus execute with greater power and confidence

Therefore, this chapter looks at decision making through the data and information lens. This chapter discusses how good decision makers manage the uncertainty that is inherent in decision making by informationalizing the entire process. Finally, it notes a dark side of the Information Age: however off-the-wall a decision may be, rest assured that there are plenty of data and information that support it.

Decisions Through the Data and Information Lens

Decisions are the quintessential information products. The only inputs are data and information, ranging from carefully researched hard facts to tacit information in its many gradations, from anecdotes that capture the essence of some aspect of the situation to long-held and ill-supported biases. The outputs, including the option selected, the choice of tactics and plans to implement it, the rationale for the decision, and the predicted results, inform people and groups what they are to do next and, it is hoped, build support for the decision.

Through the data and information lens, decision making is largely about managing uncertainty and the associated penalties and rewards (see "Uncertainty, Rewards, Penalties, and Risk"). Consultants rave about "decision making based on the facts" because it reduces uncertainty, particularly compared with the ever-popular alternatives such as decision making based on intuition, decision making based on anecdote, and decision making based on the way we have always done things.

By definition, decisions involve uncertainty. If a decision algorithm could completely eliminate uncertainty, then the right thing to do would be clear and there would be no need to make a decision at all. Everyone who has ever made a decision has experienced this. It is almost always the case that some of the inputs point in one direction and some in another. And, no matter how carefully the issue is researched, something unexpected always seems to come up. The common name for the unexpected is *luck*, although the better prepared are consistently luckier than the ill-prepared.

Unfortunately, decision making is not so simple as to involve reducing uncertainty only. Consider the steps an organization might take to select a person for a well-defined executive position, say the head of operations.

Uncertainty, Rewards, Penalties, and Risk

R ecall that *uncertainty* is an individual, subjective measure. In some cases, uncertainty can be quantified in terms of probability. In others, uncertainty resides in the pit of the stomach, measurable only by the difficulty in getting to sleep. As used here, *reward* is the possible gain and *penalty* the loss that results from a decision. *Risk* combines the two notions. Statisticians combine the two formally and define risk as the product of the penalty and the probability that it will occur.

It is easiest to see these terms in action with games of chance, but I find something dissatisfying about equating decisions that can affect people's lives with games of chance.

In the first step, a recruiter solicits and reviews résumés, checks credentials, and conducts screening interviews. These provide data and information about each candidate's education, career, and other background and reduce a great deal of uncertainty. For the sake of discussion, assume the recruiter recommends two candidates, who then meet with members of the executive team. Both candidates are well qualified, so the focus of the internal interviews is not on formal qualifications as much as on intangible factors, such as how each candidate will fit in, personal chemistry, and whether candidates will be happy in the new role.

As the process continues, one interviewer points out that one candidate is an innovator and the other is not. No one had given any thought to the ability to innovate as a desirable trait for the head of operations, perhaps because there had been so little during the term of the previous head. But now they see new possibilities for the role and redefine the job requirements. At this point the organization may well ask its recruiter to redo its search, focusing specifically on the new requirement.

This example illustrates several important roles that data and information play in decision making. First, data and information do help reduce uncertainty, in exactly the manner that chapter 1 suggests. In the example here, the hard data (candidates' educational background, etc.) helped narrow the field of candidates to two. More tacit information, such as impressions about how well a candidate would fit in, further reduced uncertainty.

The observation that one candidate was an innovator had, at least for a time, the opposite effect. It increased uncertainty by forcing decision makers to widen the scope of their model of the ideal candidate. The organization effectively started its search all over, in recognition of the need to explore this new dimension. "Increased uncertainty" sounds bad, and it is a poor label for what is actually happening. Rather, new information can lead a decision maker to weigh factors differently, to recognize new options, and to frame the decision in a more positive, vital fashion. Uncertainty may well have increased, but in doing so may well improve the eventual decision.

A lot has been written recently about the relative merits of hard facts versus tacit information. Hard facts are (one hopes) the result of carefully managed processes and systematic analysis. There is something satisfying about them—particularly since they can be shared, dissected, and confirmed. But they can only go so far. Tacit information and a richly developed intuition about what is important cover areas that hard facts simply do not. They spark the imagination, enabling people to formulate new options and see the hard facts in new lights. The insight of the potential for an innovator in an operations position came from some interviewer's ill-defined intuition.

Although some may be tempted to value hard facts over tacit information or vice versa, when seen through the data and information lens both are essential to good decision making. An old saying goes, "When the facts disagree with intuition, they must be discarded," and all too many organizations treat the saying as a rule, not a caution flag. But of course this should not be the case. Used well, facts and tacit information can complement one another, as the example in figure 4-1 depicts. Even when some facts and tacit information point one way and some the other, good decision makers give both their proper consideration.

It is trite to observe that decisions are no better than the data and information on which they are based. Bad data lead decision makers astray. Chapter 2 cited the decision by the Bush administration to invade Iraq based, in part, on the suspected presence of weapons of mass destruction and the association of Al Qaeda with the regime of Saddam

FIGURE 4-1

A typical decision flow

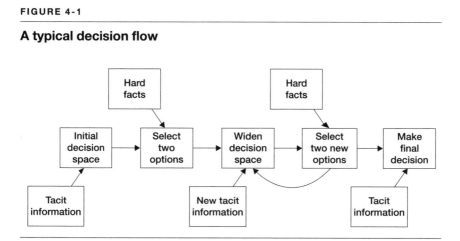

Hussein, both of which were incorrect. Another example changed the business landscape, when senior leadership of AT&T in the late 1990s trusted the falsely reported WorldCom unit costs, even though seasoned internal veterans disagreed.[2]

But these examples are simplistic. There were no doubts that Saddam Hussein had committed unspeakable acts and that AT&T's unit costs needed to come down. Through the data and information lens, all decisions involve contradictory inputs. Therefore, part of the decision maker's task is to separate the high-quality inputs, which should be used in making the decision, from the poor-quality inputs, which should be discarded.

Because decision makers cannot know whether inputs are correct, they must make those judgments based on their level of trust in the source. Sometimes a decision maker's judgment is wrong. Besides the mistaken belief that incorrect inputs are correct, the lack of trust in correct inputs leads to unnecessary delay as decision makers seek other or confirmatory data. As the saying "He who hesitates is lost" attests, the consequences can be severe.

Of course, many decisions are made under the press of time. Sometimes the most important constraint facing a decision maker is the time available to absorb the input data. Other times the most important constraint is a due date, as when one candidate must select another opportunity. And in some situations, not deciding is effectively an implicit decision. For example, not deciding among the two candidates is equivalent to deciding not to hire either.

Finally, no decision—no really important one, anyway—is made in the absence of politics. Stakeholders, naturally enough, want a decision to go their way. And many are not above offering favors and punishments to get their way.

Thus, the art in decision making lies in balancing the goals of making sure one's decision space is wide enough, reducing uncertainty within that space, weighing the hard and soft information, sifting the "correct" inputs from the "incorrect," taking political realities into account, and doing so in a reasonable amount of time and with reasonable effort. Individual decisions that result from a healthy balance of these factors are called *informed decisions*. The remainder of this chapter examines ways in which both organizations and individual managers can make more of them.

Good Decision Makers Adapt Their Decision Criteria to the Circumstances

Figure 4-2 presents a simple example involving three potential decisions, labeled A, B, and C. For the sake of the example, the decision can "succeed," prove "neutral," or "fail." The top-left portion of the figure summarizes the probabilities and anticipated rewards and penalties for each. Decision B is the classic "high-risk, high-reward" scenario, decision A is

FIGURE 4-2

The influence of decision criteria on decision making

This example illustrates how the choice of decision criterion affects the best decision.

		Decision				
	Statistic	A	B	C	Decision criterion	"Best" decision
Situation analysis	Likelihood of success	0.5	0.5	0.7		
	Reward ($mil)	2	6	5		
	Likelihood of neutral result	0.2	0.1	0.15		
	Reward ($mil)	0	0	0		
	Likelihood of failure	0.3	0.4	0.05		
	Penalty ($mil)	−1	−3	−3		
Decision statistics	Expected return ($mil)	0.7	1.8	3.35	Maximize	C
	Reward, if right ($mil)	2	6	5	Maximize	B
	Upside potential ($mil)	1	3	3.5	Maximize	C
	Penalty, if wrong ($mil)	−1	−3	−3	Minimize	A
	Risk ($mil)	−0.3	−1.2	−0.15	Minimize	C

its opposite number, and decision C lies somewhere in the middle. Presented with such inputs, what is the "best"decision?

The answer is, "It depends." The lower portion of the figure presents five criteria for making the decision and the correct decision under each criterion. Note that:

- C is the best decision if the goal is to maximize the expected return.

- B is best if garnering the largest possible reward is the goal.

- C is also best if the goal is to maximize the upside potential (as used here, *upside potential* combines the probability of success with the reward).

- A is best if minimizing the worst-case scenario, or penalty for being wrong, is the goal.

- C is also best if minimizing the risk, where *risk* combines the probability of failure with the penalty, is the goal.

As even this simple example makes clear, this is a horribly complex and important subject. It is made even more complex by the passions surrounding big decisions, as managers accuse one another of "being an old fuddy-duddy" or "a lone cowboy" because one thinks it best to minimize risk and another wants to go for broke. Importantly, these managers may not be able to articulate the root cause of their disagreement.

Good decision makers thrive in such situations. They recognize that different circumstances call for different decision criteria, and they instinctively know when to go for the big score and when to play it safe. They see the disagreements for what they are, and they are able to advance their point of view without stepping on too many toes.

Good Decision Makers Develop Sources of Trusted, High-Quality Data and Information

I have already noted that decisions are no better than the data and information on which they are based. There are two related, but separate, requirements: that the input data be correct and that decision makers trust them. Figures 4-3a and 4-3b illustrate what occurs when each of these requirements, respectively, is not met. In figure 4-3a, one of the "facts" associated with decision C of figure 4-2 is wrong. In figure 4-3b, the decision maker simply does not trust the inputs provided for decision C and therefore discards that alternative. In both cases, a suboptimal decision results.

Although figures 4-3a and 4-3b are simplistic, they reflect the situation most decision makers face every day. Indeed, according to a recent study, "an overwhelming majority of business leaders don't have the information they need to accurately assess business performance and support

FIGURE 4-3a

The influence of correct data or information on decision making

Suppose the decision maker is using this table, rather than figure 4-2, to make his or her decision and that one "fact" (the shaded cell) for decision C is wrong. The decision maker will make a suboptimal decision.

	Statistic	A	B	C	Decision criterion	"Best" decision
Situation analysis	Likelihood of success	0.5	0.5	0.7		
	Reward ($mil)	2	6	2.5		
	Likelihood of neutral result	0.2	0.1	0.15		
	Reward ($mil)	0	0	0		
	Likelihood of failure	0.3	0.4	0.05		
	Penalty ($mil)	−1	−3	−3		
Decision statistics	Expected return ($mil)	0.7	1.8	1.6	Maximize	B
	Reward, if right ($mil)	2	6	2.5	Maximize	B
	Upside potential ($mil)	1	3	1.75	Maximize	B
	Penalty, if wrong ($mil)	−1	−3	−3	Minimize	A
	Risk ($mil)	−0.3	−1.2	−0.15	Minimize	C

Above the A/B/C columns: **Decision**

97

FIGURE 4-3b

The influence of trust in data on decision making

In this situation, the decision maker does not trust the inputs provided in support of decision C. He or she will naturally discount C as an option, robbing himself or herself of the best decision under three decision criteria.

			Decision			Decision	"Best"
	Statistic	A	B	C		criterion	decision
Situation analysis	Likelihood of success	0.5	0.5	0.7			
	Reward ($mil)	2	6	5			
	Likelihood of neutral result	0.2	0.1	0.15			
	Reward ($mil)	0	0	0			
	Likelihood of failure	0.3	0.4	0.05			
	Penalty ($mil)	−1	−3	−3			
Decision statistics	Expected return ($mil)	0.7	1.8	3.35		Maximize	B
	Reward, if right ($mil)	2	6	5		Maximize	B
	Upside potential ($mil)	1	3	3.5		Maximize	B
	Penalty, if wrong ($mil)	−1	−3	−3		Minimize	A
	Risk ($mil)	−0.3	−1.2	−0.15		Minimize	A

management decisions."[3] Further, Peter Drucker admonished, "Few executives know how to ask: What information do I need to do my job? When do I get it? And from whom should I be getting it?"[4] Finally, in the headlong rush to an important decision, there may not be time to think through exactly what data and information would be most relevant, never mind to spot errors and have them corrected. No wonder managers and organizations have such a tough time making sound decisions.

Good decision makers recognize that there is no alternative to high-quality inputs that they trust. And they recognize that the only way to meet these requirements is to proactively manage their data and information sources.

For routine decisions this is comparatively easy. The required inputs can be carefully defined in advance and laid out in purchasing, expense, and other forms; and simple measures can ensure that they are correct. One of my favorite quality management stories involves a purchasing group that found itself constantly correcting errors in the data. This took time and was bad for morale. When the group stopped making corrections and simply returned the erroneous forms, engineers complained bitterly. But errors soon ceased.[5]

The inputs needed for less-routine decisions are increasingly complex, diverse, and less structured.

Good decision makers cultivate a trusted core of sources that they know will provide clearly defined, accurate, up-to-date, and timely information. Decision makers need not understand the hidden nuances ahead of time, but they must cultivate a network of trusted advisers who will explain these nuances as the need arises.

I am often bewildered by the degree to which some decision makers trust information obtained from a competitor above the contradictory numbers provided by their own staffs. For example, it seems strange to me that AT&T senior leadership accepted WorldCom figures contrary to the advice of seasoned internal veterans.[6] It sometimes seems that internal sources have two strikes against them. Perhaps these decision makers assume that insiders are biased or that theirs is the only organization that has trouble producing quality data, even though it is more often the case that known biases and shortcomings in the data provide a better base for decisions than unknown biases and shortcomings.

Good decision makers recognize that they simply must be able to trust internal data, summary statistics, and reports. They may accept comments such as, "My guys have scrubbed these data as best we can" in the near term, but over the long term they insist that those responsible follow the good-practice habits of chapter 3 and provide credible reasons why the data they need for decisions are correct.

Good decision makers cultivate a wide variety of trusted sources—the wider, the better. Consultants, colleagues from previous jobs, government statistics, academic studies, and others are all candidate sources. And of course, an executive's network should extend far beyond his or her trusted core. Said differently, executives need sources they do *not* fully trust—those who see the world in offbeat ways or who have strong opinions and are not afraid to share them.

The better part of a decision maker's source management efforts should be continual and well in advance of any particular decision. But how should he or she proceed when the moment of truth arrives? At that point the executive should do his or her best to answer the following questions for any information central to the decision:

- Where did these data and information originate?

- What do we know about the source? Is it part of the trusted core, a usually reliable source, a mortal competitor, or somewhere in between?

- Does the source have any stake in the decision? If yes, what is the nature of that stake?

- Within its realm, has the source provided all possible data and information? Or is it holding "the really good stuff" back? (Chapter 7 has more to say about this subject.)

- Are there any independent sources? Do they confirm the information?

- Why was the information collected? Is that reason close enough to the use to which we want to put it?

- Is the information merely anecdotal or was it collected purposefully?

Although few sources or bits of information will yield positive answers to all the questions, the more positive answers, the higher the likelihood that the source should be trusted.

Good Decision Makers Show Discipline

Good decision makers recognize that emotions make it more difficult to make good decisions. The recommendation for data mining software that a newly minted middle manager is about to make may be the most important decision of his career to date. He is naturally fearful that his next promotion will crash if the software does. This fear may cause him to ignore certain inputs, impel him to adopt a more conservation decision criterion, or color his judgment. He treats his recommendation as a one-of-a-kind exercise and agonizes over it. A more experienced manager is better able to detach her emotions from the decision.

Organizations that consistently make good decisions help their people do so. They know they must make all sorts of decisions every day, from purchasing software to hiring a new executive or making a strategic acquisition. The vast majority are routine and repetitive. Therefore they apply the rigors of process management when and where it makes sense to do so. Doing so helps both the middle manager mentioned earlier to make his most important decision an informed one and the organization as a whole to make consistently better decisions.

Discipline is most critical when the flames of passion and the fury of politics peak, as is usually the case with important decisions. Those who keep their cool have an enormous advantage. This is not to say that good decision makers are not passionate. They are. They care deeply about their organizations, the people that work there, their customers, and their products, and they are passionate about their own careers. But they simply understand that a bad decision won't serve any of these interests, and they recognize that it is more difficult to weigh inputs, keep an open mind, and build support when they're jubilant, frustrated, scared, or angry. Therefore, they keep their emotions in check.

Good Decision Makers Treat Those Affected by Decisions as Customers

One of the great benefits of looking at decision making through the data and information lens is that it brings "customers," those affected by a decision, to the fore. The more common term is *stakeholder*, but *customer* is a more humanizing term (see "Decisions and Their Customers").

Good practice calls for making a careful list of customers and their needs. The number of customers is usually large, including the following:

- Outside customers who will be affected

- Shareholders and owners

- Competitors (although one is not trying to meet their needs)

- Other outsiders who will be affected, either directly or indirectly

- Employees and other insiders

- Those who must implement a decision (the organization's ability to execute a decision is probably the single most important consideration in decision making)

- Members of the outside society who may be affected

- The decision maker (from this perspective, one should recognize that the decision maker is a customer of his or her own decision)

This dictum applies to both decision processes and one-of-a-kind strategic decisions. The middle manager mentioned earlier who needs specialized software so his group can make sophisticated calculations is a customer of the purchasing process. He may complain that his needs are not being met—that the process is too slow and bureaucratic. This may very well be true, but he is only one of several customers and may be rather low on the priority list. Other customers may include the IT department, which must support the new software; the purchasing department, which may have negotiated special rates the analyst does

Decisions and Their Customers

I find it interesting and unfortunate that the term *customer* is so rarely applied to decision making. *Stakeholders* is certainly accurate—those affected by a decision certainly have a stake in the decision—but the term is too clinical for my taste. Most people hold an elevated view of customers (and equivalent terms such as *clients* and *patients*). From this perspective, "high-quality decisions meet the most important needs of the most important customers," and there are many customers, with highly diverse needs, for decisions with long consequences. I think it is humanizing to acknowledge even the least important as a customer!

not know about; and the finance group, which is responsible for budgetary control. Of course, the purchasing process must also be designed to balance the competing needs. Features such as a fast-track purchase should be built in, giving the middle manager recourse if his software needs cannot be met otherwise.

Truly important decisions merit their own customer analyses. Good decision makers recognize that their understanding of customer needs evolves as the decision process unfolds and keep these data current every step of the way.

One last point on customer needs: treating those affected by decisions as customers is most important for the really tough decisions. Tough decisions are tough precisely because they cannot possibly satisfy all customers. Good decision makers recognize that people have a basic need to be heard and do their best to make sure that those who may not get their way have ample opportunity to be heard. Similarly, they recognize that a "surprise decision" carries a double sting for people who do not get their way. Therefore they keep important customers advised every step of the way. Under these circumstances, some people (certainly not all) pay back the decision maker by supporting a decision they do not like.

Good Decision Makers Rate the Quality of a Decision Based on Results

Ultimately, decision making and decisions must be judged on the results they produce for customers. During AT&T's fall from the list of corporate greats in the late 1990s, the new CEO, Mike Armstrong, introduced a strategy to reenter local markets and provide end-to-end service (much like predivestiture AT&T). To do so, AT&T began buying cable companies and working to integrate cable TV and phone service. But AT&T continued to go downhill. Many of my former colleagues refused to find any fault with Mr. Armstrong's strategy. "It was a fine strategy," they claimed. "We just couldn't execute it." (Another important factor was that AT&T simply could not match WorldCom's reported operational expenses, which later proved to be false, as noted earlier.)

Through the data and information lens, my colleagues were simply wrong. Employees and shareholders were customers for the strategic direction. A strategy that the former could not execute and that created no new value for the latter cannot, through this lens, be considered anything but a failure.

If decisions are judged on their outcomes, it follows that people must take the time to systematically evaluate those outcomes and measure them. Many managers and organizations have difficulty doing this—they simply move on to the next crisis. But without the introspection that comes with measurement, it is simply impossible to do better in the future. Politics aside, there is no reason that purchasing, hiring, performance review, budgeting, and a myriad of other important but routine decisions (and decision processes) should not be subjected to the scrutiny of systematic evaluation and measurement. Even simple measurements (e.g., what fraction of new hires are still on the payroll one, two, or three years later; what the average time is to complete a simple purchase; what fraction of budgets are met within 1, 2, or 3 percent; customer satisfaction with these processes) and analyses might well be eye-openers and lead to cost-effective improvements.

Organizations that make consistently good decisions systematically measure outcomes. Two examples suffice. Few decisions are affected by more variables than those in professional sports (with the added pressure of the criticism of national media and armchair managers and coaches). Yet the successes of the Oakland Athletics, St. Louis Cardinals, New England Patriots, and others that systematically measure the results of personnel and game-day decisions testify to the power of doing so.[7]

The other example involves reading radiology films, a demanding and knowledge-intense job. Systematic measurement of decisions about the presence of breast cancers and subsequent analysis have led to a one-third decrease in the number of false negatives (i.e., films where tumors were missed and proved later to exist).[8]

Of course, the most important, long-consequence decision processes are not repetitive. For strategic decisions, major new products, and selection of new enterprise software, measurements that simply count the successes are neither feasible nor desired—but postmortem reviews are (see "Even-Handed Judgment"). A *postmortem review* is nothing

---

Even-Handed Judgment

E arlier, I concluded that Mike Armstrong and AT&T's decision to reenter local markets was a failure. That conclusion, of course, may seem unfair. After all, good processes can, from time to time, produce bad outcomes. The strategy selected could also have been the best of many bad alternatives. Finally, AT&T may simply have been unlucky.

It is important to bear in mind that a mediocre decision, the result of a contrived and ill-managed process, can also produce good results. Rewarding such a decision is just as unfair as castigating Mr. Armstrong without the facts. These two examples underscore the need for deep postmortem analysis on both failed and successful decisions. For if one simply eschews the AT&T lessons in favor of dumb luck, future decisions are doomed to mediocrity.

---

more than a systematic analysis of a decision, the inputs that helped shape it, the options considered, the factors that weighed heavily in the decision, the decision itself, its implementation, and the results. Done properly (a task more easily said than done), a postmortem is an opportunity to learn "what we should have known," "what worked," "what didn't work," and "what we should try to do differently next time."

The United States military consistently subjects itself to postmortem analysis. Even the most minor battle is scrutinized, and many are continually reevaluated to understand how tactics are affected by new technology. Battle groups of all sizes undergo simulated battles, with results examined in detail in search of improved tactics.[9]

Business schools conduct a form of postmortem analysis through the case study method, so future generations of managers do indeed learn from the past. But providing business school training is not the spirit of the postmortem. The purpose of the postmortem analysis is to help the organization that made the decision evaluate it and decide, in light of its own capabilities and goals, how to do better next time. All organizations should routinely conduct postmortems for themselves.

Good Decision Makers Recognize That Making a Decision Is Only the Beginning

The famous economist John Maynard Keynes was once asked how he responds when new data do not support his earlier judgment. He replied, "I change my opinion. What do you do, sir?"

This quotation crystallizes the way good decision makers behave. They know that a newly made decision is but the first step in its execution. They regularly and systematically evaluate how well a decision is proving itself in practice by acquiring new data and information. They are not afraid to modify their decisions, even admitting they are wrong and reversing course, if the facts demand it (see "Many Decision Makers Are Closet Bayesians").

Many Decision Makers Are Closet Bayesians

Bayesian statistics is an important branch of statistics that differs from classic statistics in the way it makes inferences based on data. More and more people and organizations apply Bayesian statistics in a variety of areas, although it is a subject of some controversy within the field. One of its advantages is that it provides an explicit means to quantify uncertainty, both a priori, that is, in advance of the data, and a posteriori, in light of the data.

Although, once again, I know of no formal study, it appears to me that many good decision makers follow at least three Bayesian principles. First, they bring as much of their prior experience as possible to bear in formulating their initial decision spaces and determining the sorts of information they will consider in making the decision. Second, for big, important decisions, they adopt decision criteria that minimize the maximum risk (it appears to me that they rate "living to play another day" above "hitting a home run" in such circumstances). Third, they constantly evaluate new data to determine how well a decision is working out, and they do not hesitate to modify the decision as needed.

Good Decision Makers Avoid Easy Traps Exacerbated by the Information Age

When it comes to decision making, information technologies, especially the Internet, have an amplifying effect. They help make good decisions and decision makers more effective and efficient. They can also exacerbate several decision-making "traps," including the following:

- Analysis paralysis

- Rigging the system

- Second-guessing

- Groupthink

Analysis Paralysis

Analysis paralysis occurs when managers and organizations cannot make a decision until all uncertainty has been eliminated. They desperately seek more information that will nail down one final detail, identify a new option, or both, despite the diminishing benefits of the information over an extended period of time. Anecdotally, it appears to me that the trap is more severe when decision makers fear they will be punished for suboptimal decisions.

Research concludes that many excellent decision makers avoid this trap by selecting solutions that are "good enough," rather than continuing to seek the optimal solution.[10] Judged through the data and information lens, this is certainly an effective process, particularly when time is limited.

Rigging the System

I call the second trap *rigging the system*. We have all experienced decisions made this way. The person in charge:

Step 1: Decides what he wants to do

Step 2: Assembles facts that support the decision

Step 3: Tests the decision and its rationale on a few trusted advisers

Step 4: Assembles more facts to address any holes in the previous rationale

Step 5: Announces the decision

Step 6a (if the decision proves successful): Takes credit

Step 6b (if the decision proves unsuccessful): Assigns blame for failure to properly execute the decision

Unfortunately, the flowchart for this decision process (figure 4-4), and that of figure 4-1, which describes an honest attempt to reach an unbiased decision, look very similar. No matter how outrageous a proposed decision might be, those rigging the system have always been able to find and select "facts" to support it. The Internet has made the job of decision riggers considerably easier—a dark side to the Information Age, indeed.

Again anecdotally, rigging the system appears to be more common when people do not question authority.

Second-Guessing

The third trap is second-guessing. One important dictum is to make decisions at the lowest level possible.[11] After all, these employees are

The flowchart of a typical rigged decision

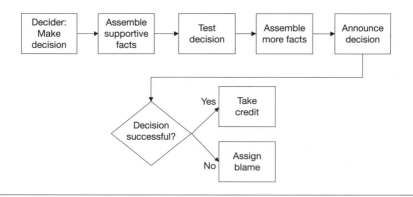

closer to the ground, which gives them access to tacit information that senior managers, more removed from the situation, simply can't have. And one of the yet-to-be fulfilled hopes of information technology is that better access to corporate goals, priorities, and policies will help lower-level managers understand context and help them make better decisions. This is a big deal. Front-line employees who can act on their own to solve a problem for a customer earn high praise for their companies, whereas those who must "check with a supervisor" make their companies seem less caring.

In fact, just the opposite seems to have occurred. These same information technologies also give more senior managers more data and information and make it easier for them to second-guess lower-level decisions. Even when senior managers are not inclined to do so, many lower-level managers have grown more tentative as a result.

To minimize this problem, managers and organizations must expand their concept of "decision rights" to "decision obligations." They must insist that those with the most complete knowledge of the situation at hand make the decision, and end it at that.

Groupthink

The fourth trap is groupthink. Groups, especially those composed of like-minded individuals, can make incredibly stupid decisions. This happens when the group dynamics keep the decision space small and negate individual tacit information. President Bush has been criticized, rightly in my opinion, because his trusted core of advisers is small and like-minded.

Good decision makers avoid the groupthink trap in two ways. First, as individuals, they keep an open mind. Sometimes it seems to me that the question "What if I've missed the best way to frame this decision?" is always in the back of their minds and sometimes in the front of it. They play "what if" games with their colleagues and staffs and are constantly on the lookout for new sources of data and information.

Second, organizations avoid groupthink by establishing a diversity of background, perspective, experience, and thought. *The Wisdom of Crowds*, an interesting and popular book by James Surowiecki, clarifies why this is so important. Surowiecki describes how the average opinion of a crowd of people is frequently better than the opinion of any individual, including experts, and how, in some circumstances, "the many are smarter than the few."[12] Through the data and information lens, the explanation is rather simple. No one individual (or any like-minded group) can hope to match the tacit information possessed by a crowd, even if little of that tacit information is shared. Individual opinions, based on limited information, vary wildly. But collectively, an enormous amount of tacit information is processed, making the average opinion quite good. So too with diverse organizations.

THE BIG PICTURE

➤ Cultivate a wide array of trusted sources of data and information.

➤ Treat those affected by decisions as customers.

➤ Select the best criterion for making a decision based on the circumstances at hand. Maximizing expected return is the usual, or often appropriate, criterion. But sometimes it is more appropriate to try for the big score, and sometimes it is better to play it safe.

➤ Measure outcomes and then apply tools of continuous improvement both to decision processes and individual decisions.

➤ Keep an open mind and involve as diverse a group as possible throughout the decision-making process.

➤ Avoid the traps of analysis paralysis, groupthink, and second-guessing.

➤ Avoid those who rig the facts based on their preconceived biases.

CHAPTER FIVE

Bringing Data and Information to the Marketplace

Content Providers

To truly earn the title *assets,* data and information must prove themselves in the marketplace. This chapter and the next focus on the marketplace demands for data and information, the many ways to meet those demands, complications in doing so, and some of the questions organizations should ask in deciding what's right for them.

The most obvious way to bring data and information to the marketplace is to develop and provide *new content.* Lots of companies already do so. National newspapers and medical diagnostics come immediately to mind, and they present an interesting contrast. Depending on the story, there is a large market for the news. But, especially with the advance of the Internet, those interested in an article don't need to purchase the newspaper. Thus, as the financial health of most daily newspapers attests, it is a tough business.[1]

On the other hand, only you, your doctor, and at most a few others are interested in your latest cholesterol report. The market for any given report is small, even though the report is easy to copy and distribute. The market for medical tests, however, is growing steadily each year.

A more subtle way to bring data and information to market is *informationalization*; that is, building data and information into existing products and services. My favorite example is the feature in new automobiles that provides you with step-by-step driving instructions while en route. Not only does it get you there faster, but also it means that husbands and wives can't fight over whose fault it is that they're lost. Informationalization is a brilliant insight, and companies ought to do more of it.

So far, I count fifteen ways to bring data and information to the marketplace (see table 5-1), and this list does not include improving qual-

TABLE 5-1

Bringing data and information to market

Concept	Classic example	Information Age example
Content providers		
Provide new content	Newspaper	Personal diet regimen
Repackage data and information	News service	Interactive data, IRI
Informationalization	Product instructions	Maps in automobiles
Unbundling	Training materials for PCs	Investment advice/trade execution
Exploit asymmetries	Used car salesman	Hedge fund
Close asymmetries	Consumer reports	Internet price services
Facilitators		
Own the identifiers	Social security number	S&P
Infomediation	Travel agent	Google
Privacy and security	Swiss banks	Privacy advocates
Analytics, data mining	Statistical analyses	Amazon, Harrah's
Training and education	Classroom training	Internet-based training
New marketplaces		eBay
Infrastructure technologies	Telephone company	Specialized database technologies, YouTube
Information appliances	Scanners	iPod, PDAs
Tools	Electronic calculator	Workflow, SAS

ity and making better decisions, both of which certainly have marketplace implications. There are several observations to be made about this table. First, my fondest dream is that this list will be hopelessly outdated ten years from now. The fun of the Information Age lies in developing wholly new ways of creating value.

That said, the table also features classic and more recent examples. As the classic examples attest, there have always been markets for data and information. The Information Age examples portend not so much that everything has changed as that demands for *exactly the right data and information in exactly the right place at the right time and in the right format to complete an operation, serve a customer, make a decision, or set and execute strategy* have accelerated and will continue to accelerate.

Third, the table is divided into two categories: content providers and facilitators. *Content providers* aim, in some form or fashion, to provide data and information specially tailored to the tasks at hand. They are the subject of this chapter.

Facilitators make it easier for content providers to do so. Infrastructure technologies such as land-line communications are classic examples. Infomediation is another good example. Infomediators do not provide content data per se. Instead, they help people find the data and information they need. A travel agency is a classic example; Google is a more recent one. Facilitators are discussed in the next chapter.

Finally, the table presents some interesting contrasts. Next to informationalization on the list is *unbundling*, which involves removing the data and information from an existing product or service and selling it as a stand-alone offering. Separating investment advice and trade execution is my favorite example—another brilliant idea. At the very least, unbundling enables a company to determine what customers actually value. It also introduces competition and gives the customer choice, which are almost always good things, in my opinion. Do you want investment advice from someone who intimately understands you, your situation, and your needs with no special products to push? It's available. Do you want to do your own research and pay low trade commissions? Also available. Of course, informationalizing and unbundling, each an insightful, executable prescription in its own right, point companies in different directions. What is going on? The only possible answer is that informationalizing is appropriate for some companies and inappropriate for others. So too unbundling.

Chapters 5 and 6 therefore pose a series of questions that aim to help companies baseline their current positions and select directions that are right for them. Managers, especially those responsible for strategy, customer-facing marketing, sales or service, and product enhancement and innovation, should use these questions to explicitly think through each of the fifteen ways of bringing data and information to market and begin to focus on what is right for their organizations.

Those trying to bring data and information to market face daunting challenges. I've already cited two: the ease with which data and information can be copied and resold and the observation that the market for any particular piece of data or information may be very small. These two chapters lay out several other issues, but stop short of providing proven prescriptions because they do not exist—yet.

Insatiable Demands

For the elite, data and information have always been critical. Those with the best data and information have won wars, uncovered wholly new product spaces, and achieved cost advantages. And the elite managed to keep the best data and information to themselves (a topic discussed further in chapter 7). What is different today is that more and more people have access to more and more data and information, and greater access has bred greater demands. Indeed, the increasing demand by more and more people, in more and more roles, for more and more data and information is a key characteristic of the Information Age.

But "more" alone is not enough. As the following example illustrates, people increasingly demand data and information tailored to the situation at hand. Virtually everyone wants to live longer, fuller, healthier lives. Health care professionals, nutritionists, drug companies, fitness centers, coaches, and a host of others have plenty of advice on how to do so. Some claims are backed up by solid science, some by old wives' tales, and some by years of experience; others reflect the pet theory of a lone individual, either a nut or someone ahead of his or her time. Consider the increasing enthusiasm, among a narrower and narrower population, for diet customized for a single person (see figure 5-1).

FIGURE 5-1

An individualized diet providing increasingly specific data and information

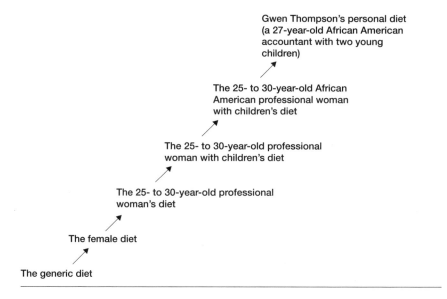

Gwen Thompson's personal diet (a 27-year-old African American accountant with two young children)

The 25- to 30-year-old African American professional woman with children's diet

The 25- to 30-year-old professional woman with children's diet

The 25- to 30-year-old professional woman's diet

The female diet

The generic diet

Increasingly specific data and information benefit both the consumer and provider. The consumer gains relief from information overload. It is much easier to consult your one best diet than to wade through the vast amounts of less specific advice on the subject. The producer benefits because the more specific advice is more valuable. Not only does it relieve information overload, but also it yields better results. Further, since the market is smaller, Gwen Thompson's one best diet is less likely to be copied and resold illicitly.

Dozens of similar examples illustrate growing demands for every aspect of the "exactly the right data . . ." mantra, such as easier-to-read formats, greater accuracy and trust, getting data exactly when and where they are needed, and information that is more readily understood (see "Understanding Financial Statements"). Some involve wholly new data. Who, even a few years ago, imagined the commercial possibilities of the human genome, radio frequency identification, or global positioning data?[2] Or the need to know how many megapixels a camera could store, or whether the green bean one is about to eat truly was organically grown?

Increasing demands, in turn, breed opportunity for organizations that can fulfill them; the remainder of this chapter focuses on ways to do so.

Understanding Financial Statements

As the financial scandal unfolded in the early 2000s, I decided to do a little independent thinking about the applicability of the data quality methods to financial reporting (they are directly relevant, but that is another story). My first step was to make sure I understood an income statement and balance sheet. I spent an hour every day for a month, but still didn't think I really understood them.

I was embarrassed. After all, I do have a PhD in statistics and work with financial services firms. The first person I admitted my lack of understanding to was a Wall Streeter, who simply responded, "Don't worry, Tom. Eighty percent of investors don't understand them either." When I relayed that conversation to a former Andersen auditor, he replied, "Tom, that guy was far too optimistic. At least 90 percent of investors don't understand a financial statement."

When I later relayed these two conversations to an investment veteran, his response was, "Tom, I think both those guys lied to you. I've never met an investor who understood those things [financial reports]. I don't even think the guys who create them understand them."

A cute story? I don't think so. As of the time of writing (December 2007), credit markets are frozen, largely because banks will not lend even to one another. They simply do not trust each other's balance sheets. It is bad enough that financial statements are so opaque that a PhD statistician or average investor cannot understand them during normal times. It is intolerable that "exactly the right data and information"—or at least "more" data—does not become available during times of crisis.

New, Richer Data and Information

Providers of new data and information are the first category of content providers. As one might expect, there are large and diverse industries aimed at providing "your one best diet." The news media provide another example. People want to know what's happening in the world, in the community in which they work, in their industry, and in their profession, and the industry serving these needs is large and diverse. It includes international newspapers such as the *Times* of London, the *New York Times,* and the *Washington Post;* network newscasts; local papers and newscasts; trade magazines; and professional journals. Internet sites meet increasingly specialized demands for news.

Many market data providers also fall into the new, richer data and information category. These companies are specialized firms that develop and provide "market data" that describe what's happening in the retail, financial, or other markets. (Virtually everyone is familiar with the stock market report that appears in each day's paper. Companies providing such services don't actually create any new content. Instead, they are repackagers, the subject of the next section.) Interactive Data, whose quality efforts were cited in chapter 3, is one such company. One of its fastest-growing services provides estimated values of less frequently traded securities. Information Resources Incorporated (IRI) and Capstone Research provide retailers with estimates of the volumes of goods sold. And AC Nielsen provides networks and advertisers estimates of how many people watch their shows.

Indeed, new-content providers serve practically every industry. For example, the diagnostics industry tests people's blood, urine, and DNA to help patients and their doctors manage health. The logistics industry is beginning to demand tracking data as provided by radio frequency identification, so that they can better manage the flow of goods from manufacturer through sales. The Bureau of Labor Statistics and many other agencies support government. They are specifically tasked with developing and providing unemployment, consumer price, and other data.

All content providers experience some common woes, which are discussed at the end of this chapter. But new-content businesses are especially tough. First, they require considerable up-front investment to develop the means to produce new content. Consider the news media. Reporting means reporters, feet on the ground where the news is happening. And not just any feet on the ground—feet on the ground with trusted sources (sources who both trust and are trusted by the reporter) and sufficient background in the subject area to properly interpret events.

The situation is similar with all new data. Interactive Data had to have a tested (and defensible) valuation methodology and Morningstar a rating methodology before they could offer their respective services. Lots of data, deep expertise, and considerable experimentation were the required prices of admission. IRI and AC Nielsen can't gather data from every retail outlet and television, so they must employ sophisticated sampling algorithms. Medical diagnostics is even tougher. One wouldn't enter the business of measuring cholesterol until research established the linkage between it and health.

Filter and Repackage Data and Information to Meet Specific Needs

Repackagers perform a variety of functions that make existing data and information better suited to their customers. These functions include sifting through (filtering) existing data and information, integrating data and information from multiple sources, and reformatting them in ways that save people time and energy. The simplest example is taking a complex table of data and producing a graphical plot, as in figure 5-2.

There is no new content in the graph, but for many people, it is easier to see both the long-term growth and the dips in the winter months using the graph than the data in the table.

Many repackagers are expert at integrating data from multiple sources. Indeed, when many people think of the "data industry," they think of companies such as Acxiom, Bloomberg, ChoicePoint, and Interactive Data that do just that. ChoicePoint, for example, consolidates foreclosure data that are filed in counties throughout the United States, integrates these public records into a single database, and provides them to its customers. Interactive Data pores through millions of prospectuses

FIGURE 5-2

Repackaging data and information

Repackaging a complex table as a graphical plot makes it easier to read and understand.

2003		2004		2005	
Month	Sales ($mil)	Month	Sales ($mil)	Month	Sales ($mil)
January	$7.10	January	$8.24	January	$9.53
February	$9.39	February	$10.40	February	$10.34
March	$8.84	March	$10.02	March	$10.94
April	$9.22	April	$10.68	April	$12.90
May	$9.91	May	$11.51	May	$12.29
June	$9.88	June	$10.03	June	$12.36
July	$10.17	July	$12.27	July	$12.45
August	$12.89	August	$12.76	August	$13.05
September	$11.48	September	$11.78	September	$13.24
October	$9.87	October	$11.77	October	$12.03
November	$12.91	November	$13.12	November	$13.54
December	$13.04	December	$13.65	December	$15.44

2006		2007	
Month	Sales ($mil)	Month	Sales ($mil)
January	$11.30	January	$11.56
February	$10.94	February	$11.68
March	$11.54	March	$13.63
April	$13.68	April	$13.84
May	$12.85	May	$13.09
June	$13.93	June	$13.11
July	$14.00	July	$14.57
August	$15.62	August	$16.12
September	$13.96	September	$14.27
October	$12.21	October	$14.64
November	$14.90	November	$15.36
December	$16.78	December	$16.92

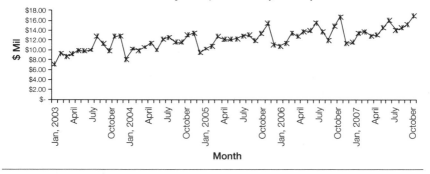

Monthly Sales, 2003–2007 ($ million)

119

to glean the key data, such as call dates about new municipal bonds, and advises financial services firms about these new products every night.

A third important function of some repackagers is filtering. News services are a good example. A customer creates an interest profile, and the service scans through articles, selects those that match the profile, cuts and pastes the first couple of paragraphs into a "Your News Today" sheet, and forwards it to your e-mail address first thing each morning. This example also illustrates a fourth important function of repackagers, namely, made-to-order delivery to the customer's chosen location at his or her chosen time, and via the customer's choice of media (note that other content providers may provide custom delivery as well).

One could provide examples of repackagers ad infinitum. They point in the direction of customized delivery, based on individual preference. And because data and information can be digitized and transmitted at near-light speed (unlike physical products), custom delivery is feasible, conceptually at least. Custom delivery embodies the essence of delivering data and information where and when they are needed, in the desired format.

It bears repeating that different people process data and information differently. Thus, format is critical. The point is important enough to merit one more example, this one involving directions from point A to point B. Some people process directions best when they are laid out visually, on a map. For those people, a good old-fashioned paper map is an excellent choice. Others prefer directions that are written out step by step. For them, AAA instructions or those printed from MapQuest are fine. Still others only want to know the next step they are supposed to take, and they want to hear (not read) the instructions, via the Bluetooth device attached to their BlackBerrys.

Further, some people are perfectly comfortable looking for street signs, whereas others prefer to be advised of roadside landmarks in advance of their next step. The list of individual preferences could go on and on, underscoring the observation that there is no "one right way" for people to understand directions. Therefore, data and information packaged and delivered to people in ways that cater to individual preferences fill important needs.

The repackaging business has special issues all its own. Perhaps the most critical involves data accuracy. Repackagers usually aim to faithfully reproduce the data they provide. But what if those data are wrong? Accuracy issues in credit reporting and at ChoicePoint have made the national news.[3] Are the repackagers liable? If yes, what exactly should the repackagers do about it? If not, how exactly should they represent the uncertain quality of the data they sell to customers and prospects?

A second issue is scale. *Mass customization* is the term sometimes associated with the business model for custom delivery.[4] It involves delivering the service described previously for millions of people, simultaneously. This is technologically feasible (or getting closer each day), but keeping track of who exactly gets what is an administrative nightmare!

Unbundling: Separating Data and Information from Other Parts of an Existing Product

Historically, when one bought a personal computer, it came with extensive documentation. Most people found the manuals hard to understand and use, so PC manufacturers stopped providing them, sending customers online instead. One result is that markets for books and training developed. This example illustrates a potential way to make money with data and information—separating the data and information that have historically been included with a product or service and selling them separately. I call this *unbundling*.[5]

The basic idea behind unbundling is simple: products and services consist of a number of features, some highly valued by customers and some not. It stands to reason that organizations can charge more for the more valued features, but not if they are bundled with the less valued features. Organizations may not even know which features are most valued.

A good example of unbundling is playing out right now in financial services. Security rating (research) and investment advice and other aspects of financial services are increasingly separating. In part this is driven by recent scandals in which ratings appeared to have been compromised by investment banking deals. More and more investors and regulators are therefore demanding that the two be separated.

At the same time, investment advisers have historically been paid on commission, when they executed trades for their customers. Consider the two features from the customer's perspective:

- Advice on what to buy or sell

- Execution of the trade

Most investors place great value on the advice, whereas executing trades is a (low-value) commodity service. But investors pay for the trade, not the advice. Therefore, separating investment advice from transactions presents an interesting proposition.

Software products also present opportunities for unbundling. Two examples are the data and process models built into database and enterprise systems, and the business rules built into so-called ETL (extract, transform, and load) tools. These components may well be the most valuable pieces of this software. They may be saleable in many other ways.

Unbundling is frightfully difficult, mostly because it causes so much fear among those involved. Consider the reactions of the financial adviser and the financial analyst (researcher). Each faces uncertain prospects when research and trade execution are unbundled. The adviser must tell clients that they must now pay for something they are used to getting for free. At best, some clients will be upset. At worst, they will take their business elsewhere.

The financial analyst is in an even tougher spot. She never had to worry about who paid her way. Now she must enter a demanding market, replete with agile competitors, an angry customer base, and a sales force that doesn't understand what she really does. No wonder she is frightened. There is not really much choice, however. One competitor can offer trades and a second investment advice, in effect unbundling the offering anyway. This is just what has happened. Companies such as Schwab and E*TRADE offer low-commission trades. And an entire industry of financial advisers has grown up virtually overnight.

Informationalization: Building Data and Information into a Product or Service

Informationalization represents exactly the opposite proposition. Rather than unbundling the data and information from the product, informationalization seeks to build the data and information into the product.[6] The concept is well illustrated by several new features in today's cars. Directions are my favorite example.

Heretofore one purchased cars and maps separately. If you wanted directions on how to get to a place, you figured it out yourself using a map. Sometimes you figured out how to get close, and then called someone at the destination for local directions. Generations of husbands and wives endured countless arguments when they got lost.

Several years ago a number of Internet sites, such as MapQuest, sprang up to help. You could type in your destination and receive customized directions. A little later, global positioning technologies became more affordable. With global positioning and direction technologies in the vehicle, drivers can get up-to-the-second directions to their destinations, recover from mistakes, and change their minds. Automobile manufacturers have informationalized their vehicles.

In their landmark book *The Social Life of Information*, Brown and Duguid note that a technology is never really fully accepted until it becomes invisible to those who use it.[7] Informationalization is similar. When products and services are fully informationalized, the supporting technology blends into the background and people do not even think about it anymore.

Automobiles provide other examples. Even as cars improved, their owners still had to worry about maintenance. One of the first advances was a little "sticky-doo" that mechanics placed on the windshield to remind drivers when next to change their oil. More recently, manufacturers have obviated the need for the sticky-doo with dashboard pop-ups that advise the driver when it is nearing time for maintenance. The diagnostics can advise of more serious troubles as well.

Still, there are limits. To my knowledge, one still has to manually check the air pressure in the tires, for example. But that feature can't be far off.

I doubt that any product is so mundane or so high-tech that it can't be informationalized. I will cite just two more examples. First is the hospital gown. Is any product more mundane than a hospital gown? I recently learned of a program at the School of Textiles at North Carolina State to build blood pressure, pulse, and temperature sensors and a wireless transmitter into the gown. The informationalized gown will mean that patients can be monitored anywhere.[8] (I am also pleased to report that the first phase of this project aims for designs that better hide the patient's physical attributes. De-informationalization, I suppose.)

On the other end of the spectrum are Dell computers. Dell is famous for its "manufacture to order" business model. But just as important, to me anyway, were the ways in which Dell informationalized its products. First was the ordering process. Rather than going to the PC or consumer electronics outlet only to be confused by megabytes, RAM, and GUIs, consumers talked to a knowledgeable representative who helped them understand their options and the trade-offs. Insights such as the following helped consumers get exactly the computer they needed:

- "If you run a lot of programs at once, you probably should consider getting extra RAM. It costs $44."

- "If you don't play a lot of video games, you probably don't need the graphics accelerator."

Second, Dell made it easier to get started. Color-coded parts ("match the yellow jack to the yellow receptacle") and a fold-out diagram made it easier to connect the computer to the monitor, keyboard, modem, and other components. More people's first experience with a PC was a success, rather than an exasperated call to the help desk. And parents did not have to endure the taunts of their teenagers who had programmed the VCR only weeks earlier.

Informationalizing existing products and services has important advantages. The markets in which they are sold already exist, and companies can leverage their existing brand identities. Thus, it is much easier than starting from scratch.

But informationalization is not without risks. The driver sent to the wrong neighborhood may not distinguish between the "directions service" and the entire car, concluding that "XYZ still can't make a quality car." The explanation that "We only provide the device; a third-party provider is responsible for the directions" is likely to stoke, not quell, the driver's anger.

Exploit Information Asymmetries. Or Close Them

Perhaps the fastest way to make money from data and information is to exploit what economists call *information asymmetries* in the marketplace. An information asymmetry occurs when one party to a transaction has more, different, or better data and information than the other and can exploit the advantage. An asymmetry may also exist because one party is too emotionally involved, is in too big a hurry to complete the transaction, or is not fully engaged.

Purists will argue that exploiting an asymmetry is not really in the spirit of providing content to the marketplace—and they have a good point. A used car salesman is a classic "asymmetrist," and although he aims to develop new data and information, he also aims to keep the really crucial data and information out of the market—especially from the other party to a transaction.

In principle it should be easy to develop an asymmetry. An organization or individual must simply assiduously study a market, develop a deep understanding of true value within the market, and seek out those who know less. Private equity firms and hedge funds seek to do this on behalf of their clients. Four things make doing so difficult:

- Others, namely competitors, are trying to do exactly the same thing. For example, the number of short sellers has climbed dramatically, making profits more difficult.[9]

- Those on the receiving end of a bad deal usually wise up pretty quickly. Thus, some asymmetrists have to continually hunt for new prey.

- Regulators and lawmakers eventually clamp down on information asymmetries. In some cases (e.g., insider trading), they take those with better data and information out of the marketplace. In others (e.g., used cars), they require sellers to disclose all they know.

- There is a business to be made in eliminating information asymmetries. *Consumer Reports*, which tests product claims on behalf of its subscribers, and Morningstar, which rates mutual fund performance, are two examples.

I find the notion of closing information asymmetries fascinating. Historically, sellers had the upper hand because they had better data and information about what they were selling than did consumers. This led to the age-old expression *caveat emptor*, or "Buyer beware." It could take hours, even a few years ago, to compare two retailers' "absolutely lowest price anywhere" claims. As for gaining information about product reliability—well, just forget it.

Sometimes it is the buyer, not the seller, who enjoys the benefits of information asymmetries. Employers, purchasers of labor, have more compensation data than do employees. Thus they are almost always better equipped in salary discussions. Companies such as Salary.com and PayScale aim to close the gap.

Generally speaking, the more powerful almost always have more and better information than the less powerful. Governments have more data and information than their citizens, corporations have more and better data than consumers, the school system has more and better data and information than parents, and so forth. Narrowing the gaps is not just good capitalism, it is good democracy.

The Cold, Brutal Reality: "Information Wants to Be Free"

All content providers are at risk that their data, once they hit the market, will be copied and resold or given away. The problem goes by the evocative name of *piracy* and has bedeviled the film, music, and software industries for years. As an example, *BusinessWeek* reports that 82 percent of the software programs used by government agencies in China are pirated.[10]

I do not think there is any real solution to piracy, although I hope to be proven wrong on this point. So far, hackers have managed to defeat copy protection on CDs and DVDs, intellectual property standards were designed for an earlier age, and the enforcement of those laws that are on the books has been weak. Perhaps the biggest legal success was the elimination of file-sharing service Napster. It does not seem to have put a dent in Internet-based music sharing, however.[11]

The risk of piracy is greatest for data and information with mass appeal. International news, the film *Titanic*, and the Microsoft operating system are all much more susceptible to piracy than Gwen Thompson's one best diet or Fred Jones's one best investment strategy. This example may well suggest the content provider's best defense: tailor-made data and information that have the effect of making the market for any specific data as small as possible. Providing content so tightly defined as to be useful to only one specific individual in one specific setting, customizing the content to the same result, and binding the content so tightly with other products and services that it can't be removed all have this impact. Demand is certainly moving in this direction. These actions also call for new economies of scale. Not just the repackager but everyone engaged in the content business must implement the technologies and processes of mass customization to achieve them.

But don't ring the death knoll for mass-appeal data and information just yet. After all, no one is bemoaning the fates of the *Wall Street Journal*, 20th Century Fox, or Microsoft just yet. Ultimately, content providers must take the observation that "information wants to be free" fully to heart. They can live with it or move in directions that minimize it, but they cannot avoid it.

Quality and the Marketplace

In the case studies in chapter 3, leaders from Interactive Data, Morningstar, and Tele-Tech Services all cited the important roles of quality in their marketplaces. Their sentiments echo the experiences of manufacturers, for whom world-class quality is now a cost of entry. (Anyone who doubts the serious nature of this point should consult the recent histories of Toyota on the one hand and Ford Motor Company on the other.[12])

The relationships among quality, cost, willingness to pay, and competitive position depend on many factors, from the characteristics of the data and information to the maturity of the market. Two points are especially important:

- A content provider usually cannot charge more simply because its data are more accurate. Providing more accurate data usually lowers its costs and improves the win ratio in head-to-head competitions against those that provide less accurate data.

- A content provider can indeed charge more for features (including more data and custom delivery) that customers want. But few customers will pay extra for bells and whistles that do not make them more effective.

To illustrate these points, consider the following hypothetical story. It begins when a company spots the need for certain new data that can help streamline logistics in widget manufacturing. These data attract a couple of leading-edge widget manufacturers, and the widget data industry is born. The market is small, but the Widget Logistics Data Company (WLDC) has it all. Unfortunately, WLDC didn't invest much in up-front quality control, and its data contain many errors. It must set up a rather large customer support group to correct the errors reported by widget manufacturers, which cuts into its profits. Customers aren't happy about the errors, but their most basic need (the first on the hierarchy of needs), namely, access to data that improve logistics, has been met. So they complain, but not too loudly.

As word spreads of the utility of widget data, demand grows and new entrants come along. Accurate Logistics (AL) follows the ten habits of chapter 3, virtually eliminating errors found by widget manufacturers, whereas Integrated Purchasing and Logistics (IPL) focuses on providing more data, streamlining both purchasing and logistics. As the market expands, WLDC initially gains more customers. After all, it's the only player with an established reputation. Sooner or later, however, both AL and IPL begin to chip away at this lead. AL better meets the next need on the hierarchy of needs, namely, accuracy. Interestingly, it can't charge more for the superior data, because customers reason, "Why would I pay anything for incorrect data?" AL does not need an extensive customer support group, however, so its margins are good. Even better, AL wins more and more head-to-head comparisons with WLDC.

IPL will attract those widget manufacturers that want the extra data. Because they are providing more data, they will be able to charge a premium over WLDC, which now finds itself boxed in by more accurate data on one side and richer data on the other. Unless it changes, WLDC is in serious trouble.

To complete the story, consider two further entrants. Perfection Data (PD) follows AL's script for both logistics and purchasing data. The Have It Your Way Data Company (HIYWDC) takes a different tack, unbundling logistics and purchasing data and providing whatever is needed in the format specified by each customer. Doing so saves widget manufacturers the costs of formatting the data. It is a superior means of access from the customer's point of view. ILP now finds itself boxed in.

Note that AL, PD, and HIYWDC all have viable businesses. AL attracts those widget manufacturers focused solely on logistics, PD attracts those concerned with both logistics and purchasing, and HIYWDC attracts those that depend on custom delivery. Over the long term, both WLDC and IPL will be in trouble.

Deciding What's Right for Your Business

The difficulties discussed throughout this chapter aside, organizations need not ask themselves "Should we get in the content business?" They are already in it. Every organization, be it a company or a government agency, public or private, high-tech or low-tech, customer-focused or internally driven, sends data and information outside its walls and into the public domain every day. Even the most secretive, Industrial Age organization provides product specifications and pricing data to prospects; delivery information, installation instructions, and invoices to customers; and reports to regulators and the financial community. These data and information may not be money makers, but it is naïve to think they do not affect market position.

Further, as I've repeatedly stressed, the demands for data and information are, for all practical purposes, insatiable. All by itself, this makes the content business attractive—and the content business can be extremely profitable. Recall that by 2010, 50 percent of the value of delivering a shipping container will be in the data and information associated with the container. Examples in this chapter further bolster this argument.

Thus, the question organizations must ask is not "Should we be in the content business?" but "What is our content strategy?" This chapter concludes with a series of questions aimed at helping companies identify three areas that can form the basis of such a strategy. Most important is the sweet spot that lies at the confluence of market demand and opportunities, marketable data and capabilities, and technical and quality readiness. It demands immediate attention.

The first three questions aim to help identify market demand and opportunities:

1. *"What data and information are we already bringing to the market-place and how are we doing so?"* As noted earlier, all organizations put data and information in the market. Answering this question simply forces you to be explicit about what, exactly, you are already doing.

2. *"What are the leaders and upstarts in our industry doing to bring data and information to bear in the marketplace?"* This question specifically directs your attention to the leaders in your industry and to the upstarts, the individuals or organizations just below the radar with the offbeat perspectives, the fresh ideas, and the passion to find a niche. Answering this question forces you to be explicit about what, exactly, others are already doing and attempting to do. The most important part of the answer involves identifying what the leaders and upstarts are doing that you are not and leads to deeper analysis in addressing the follow-up question, "What do they know that we do not?"

3. *"What data and information do our leading-edge customers already know they need?"* This question builds on the first two. It is harder to answer, because you have to sit down with leading-edge customers; get them to elucidate, speculate, and even pontificate on what they would like to achieve; and then translate their visions into data and information. Most leading-edge customers are happy to open up once they know you are not trying to hit them up for more money. The most important part of the answer involves identifying what customers need that you are not providing.

Taken together, the answers to these questions clarify the market demand and opportunities.

Whereas the first three questions focus externally, the next three focus internally. They aim to clarify your marketable data and capabilities.

4. *"Which of our data and information (including those of our business partners) might have value in the marketplace?"* Answering this question involves working through your data and information and asking who might pay good money for them (in one form or another). As an example, within days after moving into a new house, homeowners are deluged with offers for credit cards, appliances, furniture, and lawn care. The mortgage company has sold the relevant data to anyone who thinks you are a likely buyer. It has found customers for data it has to create and process anyway.

5. *"What special skills for creating, processing, and utilizing data and information do we already possess?"* This is an especially important question because sustainable content businesses are built not on having data and information that others want, but on the ability to produce more of what others want each day. One way to answer this question, at least partly, is to work through the data and information skills implied by your core competencies. For example, if your core competency involves seeing investment opportunities that others do not, you are probably pretty good at uncovering and exploiting information asymmetries. Beyond core competencies, the answers may prove surprising. "We're pretty good at putting components together" may point the way toward informationalization, and "We're good at customizing reports" may point the way toward repackaging.

6. *"What do we know that no one else does, and who would care?"* This important follow-up question aims to clarify the special marketable knowledge that you have not yet turned into data and information.

The intersection of marketplace opportunities and marketable data and capabilities demands detailed attention. There's a need and you can fill it. Before charging off, however, you must determine whether you have the required technical capabilities and make sure that your data can withstand the rigors of the marketplace. To do so, answer the following questions:

7. *"Are the data and information to be exposed in the marketplace of sufficient quality?"* People inside your company are used to shortcomings in your data. They understand the data deeply and have developed work-arounds to accommodate the errors they find. You can't expect customers to have the same knowledge or to accommodate your errors. Thus, this question requires you to think through whether you and your partners' data can withstand the withering scrutiny of the marketplace.

8. *"Do we have the technological infrastructure to get started?"* Bringing data and information to the marketplace requires a suitable technological infrastructure. Selling data requires the means to deliver data to customers, repackaging may require interconnectivity with sources, and informationalization may require robust transaction capabilities. This question forces you to think through your technical capabilities to deliver.

Figure 5-3 brings the three lines of questioning together. Hopefully, the quality and technical limitations aren't too severe and the sweet spot is large. This situation merits a specific "go to market" plan, developed by answering the following question:

9. *"How should we exploit the confluence of market demand, marketable data and capabilities, and our readiness?"*

For organizations that have yet to systematically think about data and information markets, the sweet spot is likely to be small. But even organizations enjoying large sweet spots should follow up, asking one more question:

10. *"What should we do to expand the sweet spot?"* Two areas of figure 5-3 are especially interesting. First is the area where there are market demands and opportunities and marketable capabilities, but quality or technical capabilities are lacking. For this area, the follow-up question is "How should we improve our quality or technical capabilities or both to exploit the intersection of mar-

FIGURE 5-3

Deciding what is right for one's business

An organization's content strategy stems from the confluence of market demands and opportunities, marketable data and capabilities, and quality and technology readiness.

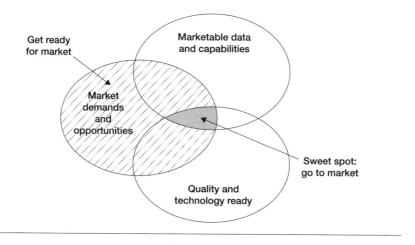

ket demand and marketable capabilities?" The second important area is where there is demand, but the organization lacks marketable data or capabilities. Here the follow-up question is "What data or technical capabilities or both should we develop?" The answers to these two follow-up questions form the basis of the "get ready for market" plan.

THE BIG PICTURE

➤ There are a minimum of six ways to bring data and information directly to market: new content, repackaging, unbundling, informationalization, exploiting asymmetries, and closing asymmetries.

➤ As a practical matter, no matter what your organization sells, at least some of its data and information are exposed in the marketplace. We are all content providers.

➤ Although any content business is fraught with difficulty, the demand for data and information has been growing for hundreds of years and will only continue to grow. Increasingly, however, the demand is for data and information ideally suited to the tasks at hand.

➤ Talk to your leading-edge customers about their perception of the data and information they receive from you, however they receive it. Ask them which add most value and how they do so. Find out what other data and information they could use and how they could use them.

➤ Review your products and services to determine how they fit with the mid- and long-term data and information needs of your customers.

➤ Similarly, figure out which of your data and capabilities are unique and have value in the marketplace.

➤ Subject everything to the following tests:

  – Can we sell it?

  – Can we repackage it?

  – Can we unbundle it?

  – Can we informationalize it?

  – Can we use it to create an asymmetry?

  – Can we close asymmetries created by others?

CHAPTER SIX

Bringing Data and Information to the Marketplace

Facilitators

Table 5-1 listed nine specific categories of facilitators, that is, those that help others use data and information more effectively. They are the subject of this chapter. Although much of the focus is on the help that facilitators provide content providers in bringing data and information to market, facilitators do much more. They help decision makers find the data and information they really need, uncover hidden gems in the organization's mounds of data, and provide the infrastructure technologies needed to store, process, and communicate data and information. Indeed, as noted in the introduction, the ongoing advance and penetration of information technologies has made them indispensable to every organization and facilitated the recognition that data and information are indeed assets.

Importantly, some facilitators go even further, enabling businesses to conceptualize their processes and organizations in entirely new ways.

Successful reengineers, for example, often find that earlier processes were designed around the limitations of a previous generation of information technology. A newer technology allows them to reconceptualize processes, meeting customer needs better, faster, and at lower cost. Although reengineering has a bad name in some circles, organizations have reengineered thousands of processes successfully since the concept was popularized by Michael Hammer in 1990.[1] This chapter highlights several current opportunities.

Further, there are many cases in which content and an underlying technology are bound up with one another. My favorite new toy, my iPod, is a good example. When it first came out, I used it and my computer to repackage my entire collection of CDs into a single device. As a consultant, I travel a fair amount. The iPod meant I didn't have to select a small amount of music to take with me in advance. I simply tossed my iPod in my briefcase. Later I started to do the same with movies. Who knows how I'll use it next? In the language of this chapter, my iPod is an information appliance that facilitated me repackaging my music and movies. The appliance and the repackaging are inseparable.

Market Scan

Just as the needs of a fighting army drive the needs for supply, so too the needs of those who use and exploit data and information drive the needs for facilitators. I've already noted that demands for "exactly the right data and information . . ." are insatiable. It follows that the demands on facilitators are insatiable as well. On this basis alone, one can confidently predict bright futures for those facilitators who align with the marketplace needs for data and information.

Magnetic resonance imaging (MRI) is a case in point. Physicians order MRIs for their patients when they need detailed images of the site of injury or disease inside a patient's body. The content consists of the images, their interpretation, and the reports provided patients and the physicians who order them, and requires the following facilitators:

- The MRI scanner, an example of what is called an *information appliance* in this chapter

- *Training* for the technicians who operate the scanner and the radiologists who interpret the results

- *Infrastructure technologies* to store images for later use and to transmit them wherever they are needed, as for example, when one radiologist seeks the opinion of a second

- Policy and associated procedure to ensure that patients' *privacy rights* are protected

- Capabilities to find and retrieve the images if they are needed at a later time, a form of what is called *information mediation* in this chapter

- Technical and process capabilities to ensure that an image is *uniquely identified* with the correct patient

- Capabilities to systematically compare images for changes, a form of what is called *data mining* in this chapter

- *Tools* to schedule patients and otherwise operate the MRI business (or laboratory) efficiently

- Some means of establishing the cost and payment arrangements for the MRI images—the *market* for the images, in other words

The MRI example illustrates two other points about the evolving market for facilitators. First is the high degree of specialization implicit in many of the listed items. The MRI scanner is not a general-purpose device. You can't use it for a computerized tomographic (CT) scan. And although the underlying technology doesn't much care whether it is used to scan a human body or the Shroud of Turin, it is specifically designed for humans. There are exceptions, of course. High-speed communications links are equally capable of transmitting MRI images, CT scans, and anything else that can be digitized. But generally speaking, more specific data and information require more specialized facilitators.

Second is the enduring need for connectivity in every direction. This is old news. Authors such as Negroponte, Cairncross, Dyson, and Friedman have celebrated the penetration of communications technologies and the advantages that result.[2] But much work remains. Even today, many patients lug their MRI images with them from one doctor to the next. That day should be long past.

The chapter's exploration of each of the nine categories of facilitators begins with information mediation, because Google, a modern-day info-mediator, generates so much attention.

Information Mediation

For consumers, the most difficult step in deciding which product to purchase is often obtaining the data and information they need to evaluate their options. As noted earlier, knowledge workers, that elusive category of people who create the most value in the Information Age, spend up to 30 percent of their time searching for the data and information they need to do their jobs.[3] These tasks continue to grow more difficult as the worldwide economy grows and as more and more data and information become available. Tools, processes, and other products that make searches faster, easier, and more effective find ready audiences.

Information mediation, or simply *infomediation*, comes in many forms and has a long and storied history. Today, people are most excited about Google and its competitors. Searchers input a keyword or two and fractions of a second later receive a long list of sites, indexed according to Google's proprietary algorithms, that point the requester in the direction of the data and information they seek.[4]

Prior to search engines, people relied on brokers or agents, many of them really salespeople, to get them the data and information they needed. Indeed, before the Internet, it took several calls to airlines or a travel agent simply to find out when flights to Las Vegas left the New York area. Similarly, home buyers had to rely on realtors to find out which homes were for sale, and music buffs had to go to the electronics store to get the specs on a new stereo system. Most of that information is now available with a few keystrokes (see "I Want a Better Internet Browser").

Travel agents are classic human infomediators. The Internet has battered travel agencies, and thousands have gone out of business. But good travel agents provide a service the Internet cannot. One recently told me that she was sending one of her clients to a three-day cooking school in Tuscany. The client could have researched cooking schools himself using

---

I Want a Better Internet Browser

I love the Internet when I know exactly what I'm looking for. And it's just fine when I have a pretty good idea. I use a browser that narrows the field quickly, and I usually find what I want in a few minutes.

But I don't like it at all when I have only a vague idea of what I want. Then the Internet simply doesn't compare to a good bookstore or hardware store. I can take in far more information and narrow my search far more quickly and accurately just walking around a physical store. The Internet's bandwidth is just too low in these situations. Perhaps someday someone will combine virtual reality and the Internet in such a way that I can feel as if I were perusing Borders from my office.

---

the Internet. It simply never occurred to him. The real value provided in this example was helping the traveler figure out what data and information he needed, not simply locating it.

Infomediation also calls to mind the general librarians of public libraries, corporate historians, and managers of some types of metadata. Librarians provide a great example of the third value-added service of information brokers—namely, organizing materials to make them easier to find.

Finally, even if all the needed data and information are readily available, many people already suffer from overload and have no time to seek out what they need. Trusted infomediators, with their specialized knowledge of a subject area, can help people more easily, reliably, and cheaply find the content they really need.

Infomediation is a fascinating business and one that is evolving rapidly. One feature that makes the industry tough is the fact that infomediators do not usually get paid for locating the needed data and information. Rather, travel agents, realtors, and electronics salesmen get paid when they "make the sale," and search engines generate income when searchers click over to advertisers' Web sites. That blurs the answer to the question "Who exactly is the customer?" This is always a dangerous situation, because satisfying one customer can be difficult enough.

Worse, it may lead infomediators to constrain their thinking about their market opportunities. For example, in July of 2007, *BusinessWeek* reported projected spending of $60 billion on search marketing over the next four years.[5] This would make an attractive market, to be sure, but I think that a better estimate of the size of the search market is the cost of 30 percent of knowledge workers' time spent searching for the data and information they need. That amounts to trillions of dollars per year. But people are used to getting search results for free and may be disinclined to pay.

However measured, there are enormous potential for infomediators. Like everything else in the world of data and information, search engines are becoming more focused. For example, Health-care-search .com, Spock.com, and Searchguide.net focus on health care, people searches, and more specific searches, respectively. More sophisticated search engines are sprouting up to serve specialized business needs, such as a legal department's e-discovery. Focus enables these companies to employ different search engines, better tailored to the needs of those who use them.

The virtues of specialization also hold the key for the future of human infomediators. People can find the commodity data themselves, and thus it is easy to predict the demise of human infomediators. But I think such prediction is off base because the deeper insights—the subtle points that are yet to, and may never, wind their way onto the Internet—will remain the province of humans. Indeed, many human infomediators find that the Internet actually makes them more effective. They spend less of their time answering routine questions and more utilizing their deeper, more valuable, skills.

Own the Identifiers

Most countries have some means to identify their citizens, if for no other reason than so they can deliver health insurance and other benefits. The United States employs social security numbers; the United Kingdom, national insurance numbers; and Belgium, national numbers.

Similarly, commercial organizations need to identify their customers, products, employees, and indeed, everything of importance. For example, a consumer goods company seeking to distribute its products via retail outlets needs to know where potential retailers are located, their specialties, how big they are, who owns them, who frequents them, and a myriad of other details. It would seem that a complete and up-to-date listing of such data is a perfectly reasonable request. But it turns out there are over half a million retail establishments in the United States alone, with retail outlets going in and out of business all the time. And that just counts physical locations! The Internet is redefining what a retail establishment is. Thus, maybe developing and keeping such a list complete, up-to-date, and accurate is not so simple.

Similarly, those selling bonds need a list of available bonds, details such as what they pay and when, who's backing them, tax consequences, and so forth—another perfectly reasonable need that is more complicated to meet than it might first appear. There are nearly a million and a half United States–based bonds. Like retail outlets, bonds come and go all the time: new ones are introduced every day, some bonds mature, others are called, companies merge, and so forth.

Both examples concern market data; that is, data about markets, marketplaces, and what is for sale. They also illustrate an important niche—the identifiers associated with content. For organizations to make use of the data associated with retail outlets or securities, they must be able to uniquely identify each retail outlet or security. The identifiers, then, are especially important, and "owning" them provides a unique, sustainable opportunity. Trade Dimensions and Standard & Poor's provide the identifiers for retail outlets and North American securities, respectively.

Actually, "owning the identifiers" may not always be fully correct. In some cases, the opportunity lies in owning the convention by which identifiers are assigned. It is tempting to view "identifiers" as a technical feature of database design, which of course they are. Organizations assign internal identifiers to their customers and products. To be saleable, identifiers must become the industry convention (the word *standard* is reserved for conventions that are developed and promulgated through formal standards-setting bodies or processes). Then, those owning the identifiers can enjoy a monopoly in their niche. To thwart this, many industries form standards bodies and nonprofit groups to define and administer identifiers. The stock-keeping unit (SKU) symbol is a good example.

Analytics and Data Mining: Uncovering and Leveraging Hidden Nuggets of Insight in Data and Information

The January 23, 2006, cover of *BusinessWeek* boldly proclaimed "Math Will Rock Your World!" The article gives a number of real-world examples, from search engines (Google, Yahoo) to routing news articles (Inform Technologies) and poring through customer records to uncover new marketing opportunities (Harrah's Entertainment, Amazon, Gatorade). The best sellers *Super Crunchers* by Ian Ayres and *Competing on Analytics: The New Science of Winning* by Tom Davenport and Jeanne Harris provide many more examples.[6] These cases embody the spirit of putting data to work to better understand customers, maximize revenue, and improve operations.

I use the term *data mining* to refer to the tools and techniques for uncovering hidden nuggets in data, and *analytics* to mean the end-to-end process of preparing the data, mining them, and leveraging the resulting insights internally and in markets. Although analytics, data mining, and the people employing them have a certain cachet at the moment (despite a drawback discussed in "The Lost Art of Small-Scale Experimentation"), they are not fads. Quite the opposite. The underlying processes and techniques have deep roots in scientific and management practice. A body of statistical methods has grown up to assist science by providing experimental designs for testing theory, analytic methods for understanding the data that result from experiments, and mathematical underpinnings for drawing logical inferences from the analyses. Similarly, good managers have always wanted to gain deeper and deeper insights into what is happening in their organizations, factories, and markets. Although they may have lacked the quantities of data and sophistication of their scientific brethren, they certainly did not lack the desire. Today's computing power, high-powered tools, and sheer quantities of available business data stored electronically provide them all the technical horsepower they need.

Analytics may be the trickiest of the opportunities discussed in this chapter. On the one hand, no organization can ignore it. The potential is just too great, and competitors are almost certainly hard at work on

---

The Lost Art of Small-Scale Experimentation

Although the notion of mining vast quantities of data and information for hidden nuggets is, rightly in my opinion, generating excitement, I fear that the knack of small industrial experimentation is being lost. Although I have no hard statistics, I suspect that the vast majority of questions don't require lots of data. As evidence, I cite all of human progress until 1940, before the advent of large computers made it possible to even contemplate data mining.

Small-scale industrial experimentation usually starts with a fairly well-defined question, such as "What if we approached college students differently?" or "What if we made the packaging red?" The next step is to find a small amount of existing data, maybe for students at one college or another instance in which the packaging was red. If those data look promising, they are used to sharpen the focus and define a small experiment. The most frequent results are either of the following:

- "That's a dumb idea. Let's work on something else."

- "That's a great idea. Let's start engaging management."

I think companies should do more small-scale experiments, even though they lack the sex appeal of data mining.

---

this opportunity. On the other hand, data mining is devilishly difficult. Data miners prefer long histories of good, clean data from a variety of sources. Preparation therefore requires a significant investment, because disparate data from across the organization must be obtained, aligned, and organized into a suitable analytic environment, typically a data warehouse. Dirty data require cleansing, which is a difficult, time-consuming, and expensive proposition all by itself (and another reason that organizations should adopt the ten habits of chapter 3).

There are many data mining techniques, from multivariate statistical methods to Bayesian methods, neural networks, predictive analysis, optimization, and so on. But one cannot simply launch a data mining application before going home at night and read the results in the next morning's e-mail. Indeed, "Data do not give up their secrets easily. They have to be tortured to confess."[7]

At its core, data mining is specialist work, requiring a deep understanding of the data, the inner working of the tools employed, a certain quantitative knack, and, often, a contrarian disposition. Many of the people who are good at it have advanced degrees. The best ones have a keen sense for the organization's customers, products, and markets and communicate easily with the managers who will put their insights to use. Good data miners are in short supply.

Finally, having discovered a nugget, the organization must put it to use. This can be the most difficult step. All new ideas encounter resistance, but those resulting from data mining are especially offbeat and unexpected. They often challenge the conventional wisdom, forcing managers and departments to reexamine their core beliefs. The net result is that aligning people can take even longer and be more arduous and frustrating. Second, the data miners' discoveries must pass *market*, not *scientific*, scrutiny. Scientists aim to discover fundamental truths about reality. They hope their conclusions will stand the test of time. Data miners have a different standard—simultaneously easier and more difficult. Their conclusions need not stand the test of time or even last very long, but they must make money in the marketplace.

Thus, data mining is not for the faint of heart (see "An Uncertain Future for Analytics and Data Mining"). To get over these hurdles, organizations should manage analytics as a big-P process, paying particular attention to building communications between the technical and business communities. The closer together these two communities work, the more relevant the data miners' discoveries and the faster the newly discovered insights are put to use.

Analytics is very much at the top end of the business intelligence (BI) spectrum. One way to ease the way into analytics is to focus first on the lower end of the spectrum, that is, on reporting. Organizations and managers have always depended on the reporting process—including standard reports, ad hoc queries, drill-down capabilities, and, more recently, balanced scorecards—to plan, set budgets, and keep their

An Uncertain Future for Analytics and Data Mining

From time to time, I fear that analytics and data mining could endure the same fate as reengineering. Like analytics and data mining, reengineering is a management tool of stunning power when used properly. In its early days, it yielded some rather remarkable successes and grew in popularity. But in time it became the management fad du jour and gained a poor reputation. I once heard a colleague joke that his wife had asked him to reengineer the lighting in their kitchen. She just wanted him to change a lightbulb that had burned out.

Reengineering projects failed not because of some shortcoming in the method, but because managers failed to understand "process" and lacked the courage to make radical change. It is too bad, really. Many processes still need to be reengineered.

We have not even begun to understand the potential for analytics and data mining. Yet its reputation may be sullied, in some companies anyway, by half-hearted efforts that don't produce extraordinary results. Just as it is generally considered unwise to put in only enough energy to leap halfway across a stream, so too with analytics and data mining.

Further, data mining is not without risks. As discussed fully in chapter 7, rules, regulations, and customs regarding privacy are far from settled. It may turn out that a company must secure written permission before mining personal data. Witness, for example, the recent furor over the U.S. government's use of data mining in the fight against terrorism.[8]

organizations on track. But too often there has been a "set 'em and forget 'em" attitude to metrics. The metrics were defined long ago, and not to capture some essential feature of the business, but because they were all that data and computational limitations permitted. A careful review will force the organization to dig down in new ways (the very spirit of data mining!) and yield new insights into day-in, day-out business performance— not to mention better metrics and BI.

Privacy and Security

I highlight privacy and security as a separate area of opportunity to heighten the importance of these issues, although I hope (perhaps unrealistically) these opportunities will not grow without end. At the time this was written, both privacy and security were front-page news items. The top-line issues are quite simple: With respect to security, too much data have been lost or stolen (too easily, in my opinion), putting millions of people at risk of identity theft. With respect to privacy, it is not clear what rights one has to decide who may use what data about oneself, the circumstances under which they may use it, how they may do so, and for what purposes.

Any organization that holds sensitive data is a potential customer for better security. A perfect solution must let the good guys in without too much trouble, keep the bad guys out, help the authorities catch the bad guys, deal with any breaches or other problems quickly and effectively, and evolve quickly as the bad guys change tactics. It no doubt includes policy, process, and hardware and software components (see "Sensitive Data on Laptops"). But, of course, there *is* no perfect solution. In fact, just the opposite. A company that is so secure that no bad guys can get in probably cannot conduct business at all. Thus, there is a need for services that help companies evaluate the risks and set courses of actions that balance these risks against the total cost of countermeasures.

Companies such as Equifax, Experian, and TransUnion already provide credit monitoring services that aim to help consumers detect threats to their digital identities in (more or less) real time. Although this is a good step in the right direction, much more is needed. Victims of identity theft can lose their jobs, their homes, and their sanity, and putting their lives back together can take years.

I think the situation for privacy is even trickier, and I'll discuss it at some length in the next chapter. It is an unsettled area of law, and attorneys and privacy advocates will have lots of work for years to come. Even keeping track of the law that affects a company will be an enormous task, but it will be nothing compared with following all the applicable laws.

Sensitive Data on Laptops

I find it amazing that organizations allow social security numbers to be stored on laptop computers, thumb drives, and other devices that are so easily carried out the door. It strikes me as the equivalent of a high school student leaving his wallet on the locker room bench while taking a shower after gym class. The thief may be punished, but one can hardly condone the behavior that put the wallet at risk.

Certainly, securing laptop computers is but a fraction of the overall security job. It does, however, illustrate the importance of policy, process, and hardware and software to an effective solution:

- Policy that outlines rules for copying data (particularly sensitive data) and securing devices that leave the premises

- Processes for encrypting data, verifying that all devices are clean, and ensuring that employees are aware of and follow policy

- Hardware and software for encrypting data that are allowed out the door, removing sensitive data that should not go out the door, and verifying that a laptop is clean, plus utilities that prevent people from violating policy and help a company keep track of all its data

---

Information Appliances

The term *information appliance* refers to customer devices that gather, transmit, receive, or display data and information. The last few decades have witnessed an explosion in their number and variety. Cell phones, the aforementioned iPods and MRI scanners, personal digital assistants (PDAs), the handheld devices that assist agents in computing your charges and printing your receipt when you return a rental car, and hundreds of other appliances all qualify.

The range of possible information appliances seems unbounded. From the consumer perspective, information appliances are informationalized, interconnected gadgets. Attach a heat-hardened wireless device to the thermometer stuck into a turkey that causes a beeper attached to the cook's apron to go off when the turkey is done, and fewer Thanksgiving dinners would be ruined. Exactly the right information (the turkey is done) is delivered to exactly the right place (the cook) at exactly the right time to conduct an operation (taking the turkey out of the oven).

There has been sustained progress in appliances to help people take better care of their health for at least a generation. I am particularly impressed with devices that make it easier for diabetic individuals to check their blood glucose levels quickly. They are a great improvement over the previous generation of similar devices, but they are stand-alone devices. A fully connected device might do the following:

- Record the time and results of each measurement

- Transmit these data to a simple database

- Look for trends or other conditions that might be of importance

- Warn the user if something is amiss, including whether it has been too long since the last measurement

- Alert medical providers of the need for emergency treatment

This example (and hundreds of other possible examples) suggests that the market for newer, more fully connected information appliances is but in its infancy.

Although there are certainly exceptions, information appliances and content are increasingly bound up with one another. My iPod and my music are a recent example, replacing my Discman and rack of CDs. So are the MRI, the machine my mechanic hooks up to my car to figure out what's wrong with it, and the GPS devices in new cars. Further, the skills to manufacture an MRI scanner and to properly interpret the images it produces are very different. iPod software is so simple that almost anyone can load music and movies, but in most cases those who provide information appliances must partner with content providers.

Infrastructure Technologies

The next two opportunities to facilitate those seeking to put data and information to work involve infrastructure technologies and tools. Although a full discussion of these categories is beyond the scope of this book, the ascendancy of data and information affects the markets for these categories.

Infrastructure technologies include the database technologies needed to store data and information and keep them safe from harm until they are needed, the basic processing technologies needed to use them effectively and create more (e.g., operating systems, applications, enterprise systems), and the communications technologies needed to move them where they are needed. Companies that provide infrastructure technologies have grown from start-ups to powerhouses, and the tech sector continues to grow and evolve. The mantra of "the right data and information . . ." will continue to place escalating demands on infrastructure technologies. One source of escalating demand is the need for sheer storage capacity as the volumes of existing types of data grow.

I am excited about data warehouses, databases optimized to support data mining and decision makers. They grow more capable, bigger and faster, every year. Of course, like everything else in the data world, mere size and speed are not enough. Much of the new demand will come from new types of data and information. As an example, I recently read an article about advances in cancer detection that may be based on the sense of smell.[9] The possibilities to improve both the length and quality of life are truly extraordinary. And new infrastructure technologies will be needed to detect, store, process, and transmit specific smells when and where they are needed.

A third escalating demand is for greater alignment between technology and business processes. There is a bit of a chicken-and-egg paradox regarding the relation of technology and business processes: which comes first—the business process or the technology to run it? Like the chicken and egg, the relationships between technology and the business process are subtle and complex. On the one hand, many applications and enterprise systems come with built-in business processes. But many organizations simply reject these processes (as the high failure rate of these systems attests), suggesting that the business process comes first. On the other hand, there is no sense paving cow paths by applying new technology to a broken or incapable process, suggesting that the technology *should* come first.

Stating the paradox in this way betrays two types of needs: those of the process designer, who needs to understand technological capabilities so he or she can align process to technology, and those of the process owner, who wants technology to align to the current, planned, or improved process.

Tools

Like any other era, the Information Age is ushering in a host of special tools, in this case to assist people in every aspect of creating, storing, delivering, and presenting data and information. I find six categories of tools especially exciting.

First are workflow tools. These help organizations manage their business processes. As discussed earlier, big-P processes are the means by which most organizations create value. Because work must cross departmental boundaries, it is easy for some items to get lost in the cracks. Workflow tools help prevent that. These tools keep track of all work items and, when one knowledge worker has completed the appointed task on an item, move the item to the next knowledge worker. This is an important idea. On an assembly line, it is easy to see any unit stuck somewhere along the way. But with data, the lost item is tucked neatly away in a computer, out of sight and out of mind. In this respect, workflow tools manage the details as data and information wind their way across the organization to the customer. Good workflow tools help process managers schedule staff, measure process performance, and identify bottlenecks, and they may be built into enterprise systems.

I also see a bright future for tools that advance data quality management. A number of good tools exist to help companies identify erroneous data and make corrections. Many companies employ these tools when they migrate from a legacy database to an enterprise system environment. That does little to prevent new errors, so I believe these tools will evolve from their tail-end focus to become more like in-process editors that prevent errors at their sources.

I include in this category tools that help companies more easily adopt the ten habits of chapter 3. Current tools that help organize customer needs, describe the progress of data across the organization (flowcharters), measure data quality, and uncover root causes of error are not good enough, perhaps because the demand is not yet high enough. But these tools are increasingly essential. Finally, process simulators enable organizations to first design, then redesign, and then optimize business processes via computer. Although not a panacea, simulators enable organizations to experiment with dozens of factors, helping them locate bottlenecks, understand the likely costs and benefits of new technologies, and determine whether minor changes are worth the trouble.

I call the third category of needed tools "goesinta-goesouta" tools. In the database community, they go by the more formal name of extraction, transform, and load (ETL) and integration tools. They do just what their name implies: extract data from one database, transform them to meet the specs of a second, and load the second database. Assuming one accepts the assertion of the importance of connectivity, the need for ETL and integration tools can only grow.

But I am less interested in those ETL tools focused on databases than I am in goesinta-goesouta tools that help content providers, especially repackagers, deliver data and information to millions of customers via the medium and in the format of their choosing. These are tools that will transform the incomprehensible table in figure 5-2 into the pleasing graph that a marketing director likes best, size it for her PDA screen, and deliver it during her morning train commute with a note that reminds her to scan it before her 9:00 meeting.

I am generally impressed with the capabilities of data mining tools aimed at the cognoscenti. When I started my career at Bell Labs in 1980, the equivalent work went by the name *exploratory data analysis*, a term coined by John Tukey. Of course, the work really wasn't equivalent, because we might have had a few thousand observations instead of the tens of millions that today's data mining tools peruse at the click of a mouse. Still, I do not think the overall analytics process is much better today, even though the new tools are faster and more powerful. This observation suggests the need for tools that help decision makers who are uninitiated in the technical arcana of terabyte data warehouses, neural networks, and multidimensional scaling get more involved earlier—tools that better associate data mining results with the everyday tangible world of customer, products, and revenue.

Metadata tools help create and manage metadata (data about data, including definitions, business rules, locations, and sources) and are the fifth category of tools I find exciting. Today's tools support the needs of data modelers tolerably well, but they are not as good at supporting knowledge workers, who, as described in chapter 2, frequently misinterpret data and information. These workers need tools that make it easy for them to find what they need, learn what data mean, and understand the data's interrelationships with other data. Further and perhaps more immediately, organizations need better tools to meet their privacy and security obligations. While I bewail the loss of data on laptops, the simple fact remains that keeping track of where all sensitive data reside is an enormous task. Metadata tools can help meet that need.

Finally, although there are a plethora of security technologies, according to a recent survey they may be contributing to the problem. Specifically, the number one security challenge identified by almost half of U.S. respondents is "managing the complexity of security."[10] Alastair MacWillson of Accenture's security practice put it this way: "It's like putting twenty locks on your door because you're not comfortable that any of them works."[11] Thus, the need is for tools that not only work, but work together, make clear exactly what is covered, and, perhaps most important, make clear what is not secure.

Training and Education

Chapter 5 used separating a product from the training on how to use it as an example of unbundling. The market opportunities for training and education are, of course, much larger. They start at the very bottom. Perhaps half of the world's population is in no position to even participate in the Information Age for a myriad of reasons, from hunger to poverty to warfare. The focus here is on simple literacy, that is, possession of even the most basic knowledge necessary to participate.

The need for training and education is just as prevalent in the developed world, although of course the specific needs are different. Less experienced people require training on the fundamentals of communications, data and information, accepted methods for making inferences, and principles of design and development—quantitative literacy, if you will. More experienced people need training to help them cope with and take advantage of the explosion in devices and protocols, nuances and subtleties in new data, new methods of presentation, and the unfamiliar issues that the information economy brings. Finally, more and more employees are knowledge workers who require specialized training in the technologies, tools, and data and information they use to do their jobs.

In keeping with the spirit of this book, different people need different styles of training and education, delivered in different formats (e.g., classroom, independent study, Internet based) and at different times.

Define and Operate Data and Information Markets

Although data and information are bought and sold all the time, the markets in which this occurs are not well suited to these assets, especially compared with financial markets, labor markets, and retail markets for consumer goods. Defining and operating data and information markets is the final category of facilitators, but it is a misnomer, because the category doesn't really exist—yet, anyway.

As noted throughout this book, there are special problems in bringing data and information to current markets. These points bear repeating. First, companies don't "sell" data and information in the same sense in which they sell a physical product. Physical products change hands when they are sold. With data and information, however, only a copy changes hands (or, more likely, is created on the buyer's site). Licensing arrangements entitle customers to use data in certain agreed-upon ways and generally do not permit the resale of data. But they can be difficult to enforce. As noted previously, the software and entertainment industries have struggled with piracy for some time, with no resolution in sight.

Second, it is almost always the case that people seek "exactly the right data," rather than "more data." But there are exceptions. Data miners, for example, desire as much data as possible. Third, it is usually the case that new data are more valuable than old. But, again, this is not always the case. Data miners certainly want as long a historical record as possible.

Fourth, some data and information are more valuable when they are not shared broadly. A stock tip is the classic example. Other data and information are more valuable when they are shared broadly. As an example, management would be well advised to share the rationale for a change in business direction.

Finally, in many cases the customers often don't pay directly for data and information. Infomediators and brokers get paid through advertising or when another product is sold. Similarly, informationalizers build data and information into their products and don't want to separate their value from the rest of the product.

Taken together, these points summarize why I believe that current markets don't work well for data and information. Different marketplaces operate by different rules. The equity, antiques, and used car markets are all very different, with different buyers, different sellers, different mechanisms for describing products and stating price and quality, and different laws. Further, Amazon.com, eBay, and others prove that new marketplaces can gain widespread acceptance rapidly. These marketplaces have expanded dozens of markets, from baseball cards to beanie babies, attracting more buyers and sellers, making pricing more transparent, and improving liquidity. Finally, a fascinating book by John McMillan shows how markets, from street bazaars to sophisticated reverse auctions, can be specifically designed to meet the needs of the buyers and sellers, while accommodating the nature of the items to be bought and sold.[12] I see no reason that markets tailor-made for data and information would not have the same impact.

One such market, provided by WabiSabiLabi (WSL) for software security flaws, aims to do just that. In the past, "security researchers" who discovered a security flaw had two choices: take what the software provider offered or sell their discoveries to the bad guys. Either way, the marketplace is akin to a back alley. WSL aims to provide a third option. A researcher can submit his or her finding to WSL, which will independently verify the flaw and submit it for sale via an auction, fixed price, or exclusive arrangement with one buyer. Sellers hope to benefit by getting market-based returns on their discoveries, and buyers hope to benefit by knowing that a flaw really *is* a flaw. It is too soon to tell whether WSL will provide a role model for defining and operating data and information markets, or even whether it will succeed. It bears watching, however.

THE BIG PICTURE

➤ Organizations can provide content, help others provide content, or both. But there is no opting out of bringing data and information to market.

➤ Most methods of facilitation, including infomediation, data mining, information appliances, infrastructure technologies, and tools, have age-old roots. Escalating demands for content are driving escalating demands for facilitation.

➤ All large organizations must gain some experience with data mining. Deriving advantage from data mining is fraught with difficulty, but the risk of being left behind is too great.

➤ There are relatively few markets tailor-made for the special properties of data and information. This area may offer the biggest opportunity for the next Google.

III

The Management System
for Data and Information

CHAPTER SEVEN

Social Issues in the Management of Data and Information

Data and information give rise to heated passions and brutal politics. I am virtually certain that this has always been so, if for no other reason than the tendency of the powerful to hoard data and information. But I suspect that passions and politics are growing. If nothing else, the existence of more data, more needs, and more managers means there is more to fight about.

A certain amount of politics is normal and healthy. Managers should engage in spirited debates over the best ways to leverage their assets. And reasonable managers can disagree about the best point in the delivery chain at which to measure market share or how to include a data set with known inaccuracies in a strategic decision. Further, managers are only now struggling to understand the unexpected properties and potentials of data and information.

Still, one might hope that something as simple as the choice of two-digit country codes would not lead to great political theater, but it can. Indeed, no data issue is so small that a simple solution is agreed to by all. Veterans also know that it is not the hard, technical issues that stymie an organization's efforts to better manage and utilize its data and information assets, but rather the soft organizational, political, and social issues.

The old saw that "all politics is local" applies to data and information as well, and those who touch them in any way must understand the political realities in their organizations, departments, and groups. That said, one sees the dozen issues noted in "Twelve Barriers to Effective Management of Data and Information Assets" over and over.[1] The "fateful five" are especially insidious and challenging. They bedevil almost all organizations and are the main subject of this chapter. Managers should also be on the watch for the "significant seven," any of which can impede progress.

Readers expecting tried and true solutions will be sorely disappointed. Instead, this book strives for a more pedestrian goal, namely, helping managers tune their antennae so they can more quickly recognize these issues in their work environments. I present some good starting measures in the next chapter.

Sharing, Ownership, and Power

Although the issues related to power, data sharing, and data ownership are different, they are so often coupled with one another that I prefer to discuss them all at once. I begin with personal and organizational power. In the Industrial Age, those with the bigger factories, staffs, and budgets were more powerful. No mystery there—they had access to more resources, so it is not surprising that they could do more. On a personal level, those managers with "bigger" entities also garnered greater personal recognition, respect, deference, and other trappings of power.

The Information Age is beginning to eclipse these trappings. Instead, those with the best data and information are the most powerful, and more and more people realize it. Sometimes, "the best data" means "the most data." You hear evidence of this when one manager brags that his data warehouse is "ten terabytes, the biggest in the company." Of course, for data and information, bigger does not always mean better. In most situations, "best" means exactly the right data and information in the right place at the right time and in the right format to make whatever decision

Twelve Barriers to Effective Management of Data and Information Assets

The Fateful Five

1. The brutal politics associated with power, data sharing, and data ownership

2. Lack of accepted practices, legal frameworks, and traditions regarding privacy

3. Misalignment of management and data flow

4. Commingling management of data and information with that of technology

5. The difficulty of defining and implementing data standards

The Significant Seven

1. Poor understanding of the connection between data and information and performance

2. Assigning of responsibility for data quality to the wrong organizations or people or both

3. Fear of the facts

4. Unwillingness to reach beyond departmental or organizational boundaries

5. The desire to take on too much

6. Poor data literacy

7. The negative images conveyed by the word *quality*

is needed, craft the best strategy, or whatever. At any given moment, therefore, "better" may mean "more recent," "more pertinent," "more accurate," "rarest," "more connected with other data," and so forth.

Many managers instinctively recognize that possession of data and information is the source of personal and organizational power in the

Information Age. When they think about it, they recognize that sole possession of these data and information is better still. Thus, the power hungry quite naturally crave more data and greater control of those data and information (see "Data Sharing and the Sales Force").

In contrast is data sharing. Virtually everyone extols the virtues of sharing. For most people this started with their parents, who urged them to share their toys with their playmates. That lesson continues. Virtually every manager exhorts her reports to share what they know with their peers—inside the span of her control, anyway. And it is easy to criticize others when they don't share. Witness the wrath directed at the CIA and FBI for failing to share information related to the 9/11 attacks on the World Trade Center and Pentagon.[2] As discussed earlier, modern database and communications technologies make near-universal, near-instantaneous sharing of data and information feasible. No other asset has this property. Although privacy and security considerations, regulations, and good taste may impose constraints, the technical possibilities are unbounded.

Still, most people and organizations are not very good at sharing—not the really good stuff, anyway. Surely the pursuit of power is a contributing factor. It might be comforting if this reflected a relatively recent

Data Sharing and the Sales Force

The last department I would ever criticize is sales. In most organizations, salespeople have incredibly difficult jobs and do not get the support they need. That said, salespeople, especially good ones, are my role models for not sharing data. They work very hard to gather details about their customers' needs, how decision processes work, and how to position their products and services, and they are extremely reluctant to share that hard-fought knowledge with others. The good salespeople I know aren't particularly interested in power, but they are interested in commissions. Could it be that sharing what they know threatens future commissions, and that it is not power that salespeople seek but money?

trend, brought about by the flowering of the Information Age. Unfortunately, this is not the case. Those who have sought to amass power have always worked to make sure that they and only they possess the most critical data and information.[3]

Two cultural anthropologists, Robert Greene and Joost Elffers, provide fascinating support for this claim in *The 48 Laws of Power*.[4] Their book (required reading, in my view, for those serious about this topic) examines how unlikely people, such as courtesans or paupers, acquired immense power, far beyond what would be expected based on their stations. It also examines how others, in positions of immense power, squandered that power, often losing their lives in the process. *The 48 Laws of Power* consists of hundreds of vignettes, organized into forty-eight chapters, each summarized with a "law of power."

To better understand the relationships between power and data sharing, I worked law by law through the book, asking "Does this law advise you to share important new information with a colleague?" Naturally, some laws (twenty-two by my count) provide no guidance. But nearly all the rest (twenty-five by my count) advise against doing so. The lone exception is law 12 ("Use selective honesty and generosity to disarm your victim"), which I can interpret to mean "It's okay to share some data with a colleague, but only if you are going to get something even better in return. And immediately." Thus, *The 48 Laws of Power* advises those seeking to gain or retain power to ignore the lessons of their parents and the exhortations of their bosses almost all the time when it comes to data and information.

We now turn to issues surrounding ownership. I noted earlier that the power hungry crave possession of data. Even those who are not power hungry like to "own" the data and information they consider most essential. The end result is the data redundancy problem discussed in chapter 2.

The obvious solution is to designate a group to take corporate ownership. Ownership as a concept has proven its mettle over and over. Organizations routinely use the phrase "take ownership" when they ask people to be more responsible for a problem, a situation, or results. And those who take ownership are viewed in a positive light. They enjoy better reviews, faster promotions, and more responsibility. It sounds like a good idea for data and information as well. At the very least, it will clarify accountability.

Not surprisingly, corporate data owners encounter enormous resistance. Those already in possession of data are loath to give them up, and they can construct all sorts of arguments to keep their data. A frequent one is "You can't hold me accountable for results if you don't give me the tools I need. And data and information are number one on my list." Worse, the notion of data ownership is dangerous, because although *ownership* conveys certain obligations, it conveys certain rights as well. For example, an "owner" almost always has the right to sell whatever it is he owns, to whomever he pleases, at the best price he can get. No organization would even think of granting its data owners such rights.

Many data owners are left to discover their power and rights through trial and error. Many fall into the trap of setting unreasonable terms and conditions on access to and use of data. One common policy is that "new data will not be loaded into the corporate system until they pass quality controls." This idea sounds appealing, forcing creators of data to do a better job. But an unexpected consequence is that some people will conclude, "They only want data that pass controls, and ours don't. So we don't have to hand them over." Thus, important data will remain outside the corporate system.

To summarize, the notion of "data ownership" is at best poorly defined. It is not enjoying much success in practice, principally because it challenges the pursuit of personal and organizational power.

I do not wish this discussion to appear overly glum. There are plenty of leaders, maybe even the majority, who think and behave differently. Many would simply like their departments to function more efficiently. Others would like to get along with their colleagues better. Some recognize and want to contribute to the greater good. And a few find the high degree of redundancy and associated expense ludicrous. But this is not an area where managers and organizations can afford to be starry-eyed. There are too many managers who, although not opposed to data sharing in concept, simply won't put in the time and effort to do so. There are also too many managers who resist, both actively and passively. Finally, managers who've been victimized by those who didn't share think to themselves "Never again!" and are circumspect in this regard.

There is no simple solution to these problems. Perhaps we're going about it all wrong. Maybe organizations should stop trying to promote

---

Internal Data Markets

C *aution:* I don't know of any organization that has successfully tested the idea that follows!

As discussed in the last chapter, markets are often effective means to improve economic efficiency. I think there is potential for "internal data markets." The data marketplace should be carefully defined. Example rules might be as follows: "All data, unless specially exempted, must be for sale to internal customers" and "Data quality levels must be reported in a specified manner."

Although I can't really predict the outcome in its totality, it seems to me that an internal data market could reduce redundancy. The profit motive will bring buyers and sellers together—buyers because it will be cheaper than creating the data on their own and sellers because they can make money doing something that they're doing anyway.[5]

---

data sharing altogether and unleash market forces within their organizations instead (see "Internal Data Markets").

Privacy: The Wild Card

Privacy concerns are growing. They stem from the exponentially increasing abilities of organizations to obtain, share (the earlier discussion notwithstanding), and analyze data in new and perhaps threatening ways. Even a few years ago, who would have conceived that a company could use a person's genes to predict her life expectancy and set her life insurance rate? Hundreds of such possibilities are already upon us or on the horizon. The issue is a wild card, with enormous implications.

On the one hand, it seems that individuals should have some ownership rights for data about themselves. Perhaps not for data that are a legitimate part of the public record—birth, death, bankruptcy, home sale data, and the like—but it does seem that an individual ought to have a say about how and when health, wealth, and other personal data are used. Alan Wernick, an intellectual property lawyer based in Chicago, goes a step further. He advocates a "data is money" approach, in which an individual in effect licenses his or her personal data for specific uses in return for a fee.[6]

There are powerful arguments on the other side. In the public sector, some argue that mining enormous quantities of all types of data may be the best way to deter terrorism. In the private sector, entrepreneurs argue that by better analyzing a consumer's spending habits they can target their marketing more effectively, in turn helping the consumer obtain products and services that better meet his needs, saving him time, effort, and information overload in the process. If nothing else, most people would love to receive less junk mail. Finally, Scott McNealy famously commented, "You have zero privacy anyway. Get over it."[7]

Privacy is horribly complex. The best I can state the general question is, "In jurisdiction J and for person P, how may an organization O use specific data or information D for business purpose B? And who (W) gets to decide?" A mathematician would use the following shorthand,

$$W = f(J, P, O, D, B)$$

indicating a five-dimensional problem. The mind boggles! It will take a long time to develop the body of legislation, case law, social frameworks, and best practices needed to solve the equation and address the fundamental question.

Over the long term (perhaps very long term), I think the privacy scales will tip in favor of protecting the individual. In the early 1990s, I heard a prescient quote—something along the lines of: "Privacy will be to the Information Age what product liability was to the Industrial Age." As the Industrial Age progressed, a larger and more comprehensive body of consumer protections grew. Indeed, many feel that consumer protections against faulty products went way too far. They point to the numerous instances in which consumers successfully sued even though they, not the manufacturer, appeared to be at fault, such as coffee drinkers burned when they spilled coffee on themselves. To protect itself, McDonald's now prints the warning label "Caution: Contents may be hot" on its coffee cups. I think this example is especially pertinent. Whether you agree with it or not, the example illustrates that society opted for greater individual protections. According to our unnamed prognosticator, we should expect that pattern and the underlying reasoning to hold for privacy in the Information Age.

As noted in chapter 2, the recent raft of cases involving lost or stolen customer data has put the spotlight on one aspect of privacy, namely, identity theft. The roster of companies hit is a veritable who's who of U.S. companies, and millions of customers have been put at risk.[8] Taken together, these cases have brought to the fore several points, long well known to privacy experts.

First, thieves are ingenious. As the ChoicePoint breach illustrates, it is not simply hackers but also those masquerading as legitimate businesspeople who aim to steal customer identities.[9] Who knows who will originate the next attack? Perhaps someone posing as the FBI! Second, there is a thriving black market for stolen identities. And markets, even black ones, are very efficient at putting a price on risk–reward trade-offs. One must conclude that reward exceeds risk, for the bad guys, anyway.

Third, the calculus for organizations is more difficult. Preventing identity theft is hard work. It involves developing privacy and security policies, scrupulously enforcing them, and being ever vigilant to stay ahead of the bad guys. Done well, it is time-consuming and expensive. Indeed, as Gwen Thomas of the Data Governance Institute noted, "If companies do everything they 'ought to do,' the cost could put them out of business. Most organizations make business decisions based on risk as they understand it."[10]

No matter how comprehensive one's measures, there is always more that could be done. It is all too easy for the critics to point out that a company that has been hit "didn't do enough." Sometimes the criticism is fair. In many cases, relatively simple measures, such as encryption, following established policy, and checking bona fides, would have prevented the incident, or at least minimized the damage. But for companies trying to craft reasonable and responsible privacy and security programs, the certainty of hindsight does not easily translate into foresight.

Further, sooner or later added privacy and security measures make it harder for customers to do business with you. As one example, many customers find proving their identity to nonnative call center attendants so frustrating that they take their business elsewhere. This is a double whammy—an added layer of security that not only adds costs but also decreases revenue.

Finally, the damage to individual victims can be truly enormous. Individuals bear the lion's share of stress and expense when their identities are compromised, and the process of undoing the damage may take years.

In response, many governments have been and are enacting data protection legislation.[11] At the federal level in the United States, HIPAA, Gramm-Leach-Bliley, and Sarbanes-Oxley are already on the books. Variously, these acts require organizations to take further preventive steps and increase the penalties for transgression. Taken together, they are such a confusing patchwork that some industry groups are pushing for federal intervention. The federal government is also considering a number of other measures, which are opposed by other industry groups.[12]

The outcomes may well indicate how future privacy issues will play out. If tough laws are enacted and vigorously enforced and consumers punish lax companies, then our unnamed prognosticator and my prediction may prove correct. If the laws become watered down, are inconsistently enforced, or consumers seem not to care, then Scott McNealy's view may win out. A wild card indeed!

Management and the Flow of Data and Information Are Misaligned

In some respects, organizations are singularly ill-designed for the Information Age. This is a bold claim and an important observation, but the rationale is really quite simple. Almost all companies are organized along functional lines—finance, order fulfillment, product development, and so forth. The various departments and business units connect at the top. Most day-in, day-out management is conducted vertically— up and down the organization chart.

In contrast, most data flow horizontally, from one person, and department, to the next. Earlier chapters have illustrated that point many times. Data that are born with a customer order wind their way through fulfillment, inventory management, and billing. Data born when a patient checks into a hospital follow a parallel path as the patient winds his or her way from the ward, to various laboratories, to the operating room. Similarly, data born when a retailer requests delivery of a shipping container follow a parallel path to the container as it transits the globe. Importantly, these horizontal flows align with the ways organizations create most value for customers. They are the data and information portions of the value chains described by Michael Porter.[13]

The obvious conclusion is that horizontal data flows to create value and day-in, day-out vertical management are completely misaligned. On an organization chart, they are perpendicular to one another. Further, data and information spend much of their time in transit, effectively in the "white space" of the organization chart, where they are essentially unmanaged.

Lest this conclusion appear one-sided, I need to make three important counterpoints. First, current organizational forms arose to meet important business challenges and have proven themselves quite effective. With respect to data and information, the functional excellence that the hierarchical form promotes has at least one important advantage—a body of professionals well versed in the meanings of financial, product, sales, and other data.

Second, data and information don't just flow horizontally. They also flow up and down the organization chart to support command and control, higher-level management functions, development and deployment of strategy, summary reporting, and a host of other actions. This point is not to be taken lightly. These vertical data flows are critical, and it is difficult enough to make them work within current organizational structures. And of course data and information don't simply follow predefined paths across the organizations. They make unplanned turns and experience unexpected twists as they wind their way along.

Third, as noted in chapter 3, process management is tailor-made for managing the creation, transformation, and use of data and information. The concept has been around for nearly a generation, with mixed acceptance (although I know of no comprehensive studies). It appears to me that, as a direct result of quality revolutions, most high-volume manufacturing processes are well defined and managed.[14] Process management is the norm for data-intensive functions, such as credit card processing, that bear strong resemblance to manufacturing. Similarly, process management helps many companies close the books quickly.[15] On the other hand, process management has yet to penetrate most office work that crosses departmental boundaries, and it has not yet made a dent in knowledge work. According to Tom Davenport, knowledge workers actively resist the notion that their work can be made more routine.[16]

Perhaps organizations are not yet up to the challenge of separating the routine from the esoteric, making the routine repeatable, and addressing the complexities of interdepartmental hand-offs.

Commingling the Management of Data and Information with That of Technology

Adding to the woes brought about by the misalignment of management and data flow is confusion about the respective management roles of the IT department and "the business" when it comes to data. Indeed, many people automatically assume that data and, to a lesser degree, information are largely "systems issues" and therefore the natural province of IT. A Gartner study that focused exclusively on data quality confirms that IT is the most common "stickee."[17]

People reach this conclusion with good reason. First, most people access (much) data and information through their computers. The first thing they do in the morning, even before getting a cup of coffee, is turn on their computers and fire up their e-mail and other applications so they can access the data and information they need to do their jobs. This was not always the case, of course. Data and information used to arrive in a very physical in-box, several times a day.

Second, to define new data or effect any changes to existing data, people have to go through IT. IT develops the new databases, completes the technical work to define new fields, creates the applications, and so forth. A businessperson may define an informative new report and test it on her PC, but to produce it routinely and get it distributed, she has to work through IT. And the business often runs to IT when there is a new business pressure, an increase in customer complaints, new regulations (Sarbanes-Oxley, Basel II, etc.), and the like.

Third, IT often leads, or at least appears to lead, business intelligence, enterprise resource planning, customer relationship management, and data warehousing projects that promise better reports and higher-quality data (this despite the fact that the previous system did not deliver on the same promise). Finally, IT always seems willing to take on data clean-up projects, in effect assuming responsibility for erroneous data. I sometimes think that businesspeople like to play cruel jokes on IT. They do not make the effort to properly manage their processes, so they create more bad data and information each day. They ignore the problem until it becomes a crisis, and then pass it off to IT as a data clean-up project. IT can't resist—someone has finally come with something other than a complaint! There are plenty of good data clean-up tools to choose from and meaty technical problems to tackle. Therefore the department takes on a problem that, even if solved, will recur in only a few months.

There is little reason for optimism that organizations will grow out of this behavior. When computers and large databases were relatively newer, I often observed that people assumed "If it's in the computer, it must be right." Certainly the new generation entering the workforce today is less awed by technology, but they seem no more skeptical about the data and information than their elders.[18]

Data Standards Have Proven Remarkably Difficult to Define and Implement

Earlier chapters have cited poor data definitions, systems that don't talk to each other, and poor communications between departments as more subtle data issues that bedevil organizations. The obvious answer to these sorts of issues is standards, that is, agreed-upon definitions of what key data mean.

Standardization has played a critical quality role in industry after industry. Although developing standards has proven difficult and implementing them even more so, literally millions of standards on everything from oil viscosity to the dimensions of a shipping container are now the norm.[19] Even data communication standards, such as XML, make their way into common use in a relatively few years.

There are a few actual standards regarding data themselves, namely, the postal standard, UPC codes, and identifiers such as the previously mentioned CUSIP. But by and large, data standards have proven remarkably

---

The "One Lie" Philosophy

A fiendishly attractive concept is making its way around several industries, variously called "the golden copy," "a single version of the truth," or "a common view of *x*" (the customer, for example). The logic is compelling: create a single whatever, and oblige everyone to work from it.

Unfortunately, there is no single version of the truth. For all important data, there are too many customers, too many uses, too many viewpoints, and too much nuance for a single version to have any hope of success. This does not imply malfeasance on anyone's part; it is simply a fact of life.

Getting everyone to work from a single version of the truth may be a noble goal, but it is better to call this the "one lie strategy" than anything resembling truth. (To my knowledge, Bob Kotch, then at AT&T, was first to use this term.)

---

difficult. The most important reason is that the concept of a standard and the concept of "exactly the right data" conflict. The "standard data" are never "exactly right." Thus, organizations are often reluctant to contribute to their development, and they are skeptical about adopting them.

For a given organization, there is a clear benefit in getting everyone on the same page. Still, standards have proven remarkably difficult. I know of one organization that spent two years developing a common definition of *client* and reckoned it had to take several dozen more terms through the same process (see "The 'One Lie' Philosophy"). Even within an organization, "standard data" and "exactly the right data" conflict.

Poor Understanding of the Connection Between Data and Information and Business Performance

Whether an organization recognizes that its data and information are assets or not, one might hope that it would see the connection between its data and information and its business performance. Few do, however. There is a bit of a paradox in many organizations. Everyone may complain about data, and senior leaders may cite anecdotes in which not having the right data burned them. Individually, many managers intellectually grasp the larger issues. But individual understanding hasn't translated into organizational action.

It is easy to tell what organizations value by what they measure. They know how much capital and how many people they have. But they do not have top-line metrics for data and information. Nor do they have metrics that connect data and business performance. Such metrics might include their costs of poor data quality, the fraction of revenue they derive from data and information, or the fraction of their data at risk of loss or theft.

Similarly, in mergers and acquisitions, companies routinely plan for "systems integration," yet ignore the rather more important data and information issues such as "Do we define customers in similar ways?" Systems integration may well prove a major hurdle after the merger, but sooner or later, it gets done. Coming to a common understanding of *customer* is much more critical.

I think this issue may arise because data are intangible and therefore out of sight, out of mind. The impact is severe, because managers and organizations fail to see the root causes of problems and miss opportunities to expand their businesses.

Assigning Responsibility for Data to the Wrong Organizations or People

I have already noted that too many organizations fall into the trap of assigning responsibility for data to their IT departments. There are other traps as well. I don't know how many times I've heard "Oh, you're a data consultant. Let me give you this problem!" As if I wanted their problems. Of course, I have been around long enough to see such comments as a teaching moment.

Not so others. My least favorite misassignment is blaming the lowest-level employees when the data are not up to snuff. I once consulted with a company that employed temps to input important data. The process that these temps were to follow was ill-defined (my client was never able to explain it to me), and they were provided no training whatsoever ("Why should we? They're temps. They don't stay long enough to justify it"). Yet management completely absolved itself of any responsibility for erroneous data. Instead they blamed the temps, who were themselves helpless to do anything except seek better jobs. And the vicious cycle continued.

Fear of the Facts

I once worked with a client that was experiencing quality issues with its customer data. We conducted a small study of their on-boarding process, and sixty-five of the one hundred newly created customer data records we looked at had at least one serious error. A couple of brief conversations made clear the root cause—the people involved in one key step did not understand their roles. My client thus put together a one-hour training course and delivered it in one location. In the post-training measurement, the error rate in that location was 13 percent, a factor of five improvement.

This department refused to publicize its success and follow up, however. I was stunned, but as one manager explained to me, "You've got to understand. Around here everyone is expected to be perfect. If we publicized the improvement, everyone would draw two conclusions: first, that we weren't perfect before, and second, that we're still not!" For one of the few times in my consulting career, I did not have anything to say. I simply cannot understand how an organization can improve if it is too scared to embrace the facts.

Unwillingness to Reach Beyond Departmental or Organizational Boundaries

As discussed in chapter 1, data and information cross organizational boundaries in the blink of an eye. Not surprisingly, downstream departments often find the data they receive from others wanting. The usual response is to assign a small group to find and fix the errors before the department gets on with its work. I often ask these departments why they do not work with the upstream department to explain what they need and the problems they are having. But many are unwilling. "If they don't know what we need by now, I see no reason to tell them" is the common excuse. Such attitudes not only lead to increased costs and lower quality, but also lock departments out of opportunities to develop new products and services.

Data Illiteracy

Some years ago, John Allen Paulos pointed out the enormous costs, for both individuals and society, of the lack of understanding of mathematical and scientific principles.[20] Although I know of no careful study, I would wager that the impacts of data illiteracy are no less costly. Indeed, one would expect that innumeracy and data illiteracy are tightly coupled with one another.

The simple fact of the matter is that for far too many people and organizations, data are nothing more than "the stuff stored in the computer," and information "stuff I need to do my job." This attitude is not fatal, perhaps, but these people and organizations are unlikely to fully enjoy the fruits of the Information Age.

The Word *Quality* Conveys Negative Images

Although there is much culture-to-culture variation, the word *quality* has a negative image in many people's eyes. In some organizations this view is well founded. Their management has only talked about quality when something went wrong. Or people remember the last reengineering effort that did not really deliver what was promised, but cost a lot of people their jobs. These people, and in many cases, entire departments, cannot see quality management for what it is: a powerful way to better meet customer needs.

The Desire to Take on Too Much Too Soon

I find that many managers and organizations have unrealistic expectations that the issues presented in this chapter can be solved quickly and easily. I have heard managers say, "I know it took the ABC department five years to get their arms around their data issues. But I think we're a lot smarter than that. I think we should be able to do it in six months."

Other managers may make a list of their organization's top data issues and decide to tackle the most difficult first, even before they have any real experience solving easier issues. As an example, consider the following customer data issues and opportunities:

- *Mine customer data to determine which are most profitable.* This will require a specialized data warehouse, a customer profitability algorithm, and clean data. It will take three years and cost several million dollars. The potential benefits are enormous, but uncertain.

- *Improve the quality of customer data.* This will require step-by-step improvement of the customer on-boarding process. Little investment will be needed, although it will probably take two years to identify and eliminate the root causes of most errors. Expected benefits are solid and reasonably certain.

Too many managers select the first project. The problem is not that they select the project per se. The problem is that they select it without realizing how difficult it is!

THE BIG PICTURE

As promised, the issues described here have no simple solutions. Still, I offer four important points:

- ➤ Recognize the organizational, social, and political issues and study them in detail in your work environment. The issues here are a guide, but all politics is local.

➤ Don't expect people to change simply because these issues are on the table. You can't change human nature.

➤ Address small issues first. It may be better, for example, to start the development of standards with something simple, such as state codes. As you gain experience, tackle increasingly harder problems.

➤ Don't waste time and energy on intractable issues.

CHAPTER EIGHT

Evolving the Management System for Data and Information

In time, I believe that more and more organizations will evolve their management systems to better utilize data and information, improve their quality, and account for the special challenges in managing them. As one example, many will name chief data officers to lead and coordinate their data and information programs. After all, they name chief financial officers and vice presidents of human resources who do exactly that for their financial and human assets, respectively. But that day has arrived for only a few companies, and most of those named so far are not true C-band executives. Yet there is too much at stake for organizations to sit on their hands and wait. New markets, informed decisions, better alignment, and lower costs beckon, while the harsh realities of poor quality and brutal politics slow them down every day.

Therefore, this chapter presents ten specific steps that help organizations manage their data and information assets more professionally. Many, such as "Get enough of the right kinds of people involved," represent nothing more than a measured response to the opportunities and challenges at hand. And several, such as "Get in front of privacy and security issues," simply advise organizations to deal with the political issues of the previous chapter as best they can. A few, such as "Establish customer-friendly metadata processes," may be unfamiliar to many managers. All build on the ten habits of those with the best data (discussed in chapter 3), and one puts a capstone on those habits, advising organizations to tightly couple their data quality efforts with their strategic intents.

One note of caution: It took a full generation to work out the organizational forms best suited to the Industrial Age. One should expect that it will take that long to work out organizational forms fully attuned to the opportunities and challenges of the Information Age. Indeed, it may well be that new-content providers, informationalizers, bundlers, and data miners require different forms. I just don't know and in this respect, this chapter is a bit unsatisfying. Still, the prescriptions discussed here are powerful first steps.

Get Enough of the Right Kinds of People Involved

It bears repeating that data and information require a concerted, disciplined effort. An important step is getting enough of the right kinds of people involved. I find it incredible that some managers still refuse to acknowledge the demands for professional management of data and information. A massive data problem, building for years, suddenly becomes visible—it could be an imperiled enterprise system, a massive problem with customer data, a security breach, or any of a million other problems. Management assigns a three-person team of data architects, squirreled away in the bowels of the IT department, to rectify the situation. When the beleaguered three make only minimal headway, management concludes they must take remedial actions to accommodate data that don't meet their needs. Not only is the current problem only barely solved, but also it becomes harder to approach the next, similar problem properly.

It's not just crises that demand enough of the right kinds of people every day. Virtually everyone touches data and information many times and in many ways every day. Each touch presents an opportunity to add value or take it away. Assigning only a few people with limited visibility and no authority is simply not an appropriate response to the opportunity.

Unfortunately, there is no general formula for determining how many people are needed. Sometimes a large number of specially trained people should be massed for the effort. Barclays Global Investors concentrates its two hundred PhD-level econometricians on the development of investment strategies.[1] Sometimes people with a common goal should occupy every nook and cranny of the organization. At Information Resources International, the Chicago, Illinois-based provider of market data to the consumer goods, manufacturing, and retailing sector, the 750 people with Six Sigma training (in a company of only 2,800 people) are dispersed throughout the company and its global partners.[2] And, of course, over the long term, leadership is decisive.

Fortunately, it is much clearer who the right people are and what they must do, as the remaining prescriptions spell out. To close this section, I reemphasize the "enough people" portion of this prescription. Size matters. A good-sized department, of say twenty-five hundred people, that is wondering whether its data program requires three of four full-time equivalents (FTEs) has completely missed the point. The more likely answer is thirty or forty FTEs, some massed, some dispersed, and many more working to build data and information into their daily work.

Assign Responsibility for Data and Information to the Business

Of the political issues raised in the previous chapter, assigning proper responsibilities for IT and the business is probably the most important. Avoiding the "If it's in the computer it must be the province of IT" trap pays enormous dividends. Organizations should adopt the stance that data and information are the province of the business. The various departments are responsible for the quality of data they create and are responsible for ensuring that their people can find the data they need. They are responsible for making better, more informed decisions and bringing data and information to their marketplaces. Headquarters may well set certain ground rules, including data and privacy policies, that departments must follow, just as headquarters sets policy for the management of financial and human assets. And it is perfectly appropriate to assign certain roles to IT. But the business bears ultimate responsibility for work conducted on its behalf.

Maria Villar, now at Fannie Mae, is perhaps the only person who has led data programs from both IT and the business. She commented:

> While developing the Enterprise Information Center of Excellence program at IBM, I learned the importance of business ownership and sponsorship. True progress in data quality and data management can only occur when business, IT, and operations all work together to improve processes and change behaviors. All three departments have critical roles. Establishing data accountability within the business is perhaps the most important challenge. It takes a lot of hard work to get everyone to agree on their roles, clear multi-way communications, and true C-band commitment.[3]

I find that if and when the question "Who bears principal responsibility for data and information?" is posed and debated, most people and organizations arrive at the correct answer, "The business," pretty quickly. The trick is getting the question raised in the right forum and at the right level.

For Royal Dutch Shell's human resources function, the moment of truth unfolded in a series of leadership meetings beginning in December 2005. Fiercely independent, Shell units had, over many years, implemented dozens of local HR processes and systems. These met local needs, but inhibited Shell's ability to manage human resources across the entire company. Shell had just flipped the switch, turning on an HR enterprise system and shutting off most of the local systems. It had been a multiyear, multimillion-dollar effort. "Even by Shell standards, this had been a massive undertaking," remarked Mike Sinclair, vice president of HR services.[4]

In flipping the switch, HR leadership came to realize that it had met all of its infrastructure goals and few of its human resource goals. "We could congratulate ourselves because we had successfully implemented a new system and in doing so turned off dozens of systems and simplified the infrastructure," noted Sinclair. "But we knew that Shell leadership would not judge the success of the investment on that point. They would mark our success by our ability to better manage human resources." Two barriers stood in the way.

"The first thing standing in our way was simply that a lot of the data were wrong, and starkly so. If the system shows there are no expatriates in Singapore, but you happen to know a couple, then it is hard to trust the system," Sinclair continued. So HR senior leadership discussed the topic openly and extensively during its February and March 2006 meetings. "We had a lot of discussion on the topic, but very little debate. We knew we couldn't blame the facts being wrong on IT. That had to be us."

Support for this assignment of responsibility comes from one other, extremely powerful and important quarter, the long-standing relationships between automation and quality. It was W. Edwards Deming who first advised manufacturers not to automate a poorly performing process: "You'll just produce junk faster," he admonished.[5]

Thomas Landauer, in his landmark work *The Trouble with Computers*, brought Deming's advice into the Information Age.[6] In response to critics of the benefits of computerization, he studied an array of processes, from text processing to getting cash at the bank, switching phone calls, and weather forecasting. He concluded that information technologies have been fantastically successful when automating well-defined algorithms, such as targeting a missile. Unit cost drops dramatically, while capacity increases dramatically as well.

But information technologies have proven less effective when the process they aim to automate is poorly defined. Computers are not very good at checking grammar, recognizing human speech, or conducting performance reviews (at least, not yet).

In a nutshell, Landauer concluded that:

- Computerizing (automating) well-defined tasks, such as switching phone calls, works remarkably well, increasing capacity and reducing unit cost.

- Computerizing some well-defined tasks, such as replacing bank tellers with ATMs, also works. It may not save much, but it may have other benefits. ATMs are available twenty-four hours a day, for example.

- Computers are not effective for ill-defined tasks.

I like to oversimplify Landauer's conclusion this way: "There is a reason computers are called computers. It is because they are good at computing." In other words, unless a business process is well defined, it cannot be reduced to a series of steps that a computer can conduct.

Each generation of computing technologies (client/server, data warehouses, enterprise systems) has promised to undo this last point. The latest is enterprise systems, which provide their own standard business processes. But many organizations are loathe to adopt these standard processes, and the failure rate is alarmingly high. Not surprisingly, "data" and "alignment with process" are often cited as the two most important contributing factors for these failures.[7]

The most important point, of course, is that *business* processes create data and bring them to market. The emphasis is on *business*, which owns and manages the processes. Any expectation that IT can automate the business's way out of a poorly designed process is just plain wrongheaded. It follows that the business must be responsible for the data.

So what is left for IT? Plenty, actually, as described in appendix B.

Craft and Implement a Quality Program That Advances Business Strategy

This section and the next focus on the steps organizations should take to build data and information into their larger business strategies. In this section, I narrow the focus to quality. As fully described in chapter 2, poor-quality data bedevil organizations. All that improve the quality of their data benefit, usually enormously. Whereas the focus of chapter 3 was on how those with the best data do it, here the focus is "Just do it." It is best, of course, to craft a data quality program that advances the organization's larger business strategies. There is no mystery here. Strategies that demand cost discipline require data quality programs that reduce the rework associated with bad data; those that demand "one-company management" require data quality programs that harmonize and build trust in data; and those that demand customer intimacy require data quality programs focused on data that matter most to customers. As a final example, more and more organizations depend on knowledge workers to find, correct, analyze, synthesize, and re-package data and information and recommend courses of action. In many organizations, financial analysts, petroleum engineers, marketing professionals, and others spend too much of their time finding and correcting data and information (i.e., on quality) and not enough on financial analysis, engineering, and marketing. These organizations need quality programs that free up these professionals' time for the work they were hired to do.

I find that many managers enjoy theoretical (and usually ill-informed) debates regarding the optimal level of quality. I do not really object to these debates because they force managers to think about an important topic. They have no practical import, however, because quality is a moving target. Ninety-eight percent on an appropriate quality scale may well have been world-class a year ago, be competitive today, and be absolutely unacceptable a year from now.

The strategic debate that *does* matter involves competitive position. The leadership position within an industry conveys certain advantages. But paving the way also requires greater skill and effort. Thus, a strategy that places the organization on the "leading but not bleeding" edge may better suit some organizations. Still others may elect a middle-of-the-road strategy. Finally, no organization can ignore data quality altogether.

Incorporate Data and Information in Business Strategy, Especially Innovation

Just as financial and human assets are front and center in the development and execution of strategy, so too in time data and information must come into explicit play. There are three increasingly sophisticated questions:

1. Do leaders have the data and information they need to set strategy?

2. Are the organization's data and information adequate to execute the strategy?

3. Do the organization's strategies fully utilize its data and information?

With respect to the first question, chapter 4 was devoted to the roles data and information play in decision making, and only a few points merit repeating here. Strategy, by its very nature, involves uncertainty; from the viewpoint of data and information, a good strategy-setting process is one that recognizes the sources of uncertainty, acts to reduce uncertainty where practical, and weighs uncertainty without becoming paralyzed. It is especially important to raise and address concerns about the completeness, quality, and meaning of available data and information:

- Do available data and information constitute a complete picture?

- Can we trust them?

- Do we fully understand what they mean and how they fit together?

- Are there other data and information, from trusted sources, that can help complete the picture?

- Are there data and information that we have not considered that argue for a different decision?

With respect to the second question, a strategy is "data and information ready" when the data and information program aligns with the strategy. Consider a multidepartmental company whose strategy requires it to present a one-company face to its customers. Such a strategy requires the rationalization of customer data from the various departments and quite likely leads to the sticky issue of data definition and consistency discussed in chapter 2. This example points to two questions that strategists must ask early in their work:

- Are current data and information adequate for executing the strategy?

- If not, what is needed to bring the data and information into alignment with the strategy?

A few pages back, I examined the thinking that led the human resources department at Royal Dutch Shell to realize that it, not IT, was responsible for the data and information needed to run HR effectively. Asking the questions just listed helped Shell take the next steps.

"We quickly realized that what we needed was much better management information, reporting, if you will, at the enterprise level. We had to develop a common way of looking at our business and interpreting what was going on. We needed new reports, but not just any reports," Sinclair noted. "Reports that people could trust and act on."

But what to do and how to do it? Leadership charged Brent Kedzierski, an experienced executive, with figuring that out. "Hugh Mitchell [HR director for Royal Dutch Shell] introduced the notion of 'first-quartile performance' to HR earlier in 2005. We translated that to mean we needed a 'first-quartile data quality and management reporting' program," Kedzierski observed. "So my first job was to assess our current practices, define what first quartile means in our environment, and propose a plan to get there."

Fifteen months later, Kedzierski and Sinclair are proud of what they've accomplished. In the data quality arena, Kedzierski's assessment recognized that HR had solid, embedded efforts to fix errors once they had been found, but there was little effort to systematically prevent future errors. "Our people resonate with 'Don't just fix, prevent.' It's helping us get people on board," according to Sinclair. Similarly, decision makers are growing more confident in the enterprise reports. "Its quite gratifying to see, actually," according to Sinclair. "Before, too often we simply had to guess."

But both are savvy about the work that remains. "At best we're a third of the way into what is really a major culture change for HR," Kedzierski noted.

This last comment underscores a critical point about data and information readiness: enrolling people into the rigors of data and information readiness may be the most difficult step in executing a data-ready strategy.

With respect to the third question, "data and information–enabled" strategies are those that fully exploit the organization's data and information assets. Data enablement is much more demanding than data readiness. It urges an organization that possesses unique data and information, insights into connecting people with the data and information they need, abilities to build data and information seamlessly into existing products, an uncanny knack for finding asymmetries, or other skills to develop strategies to bring the resulting data and information to the marketplace.

Organizations must ask both "inside-out" and "outside-in" questions about their markets. The inside-out questions involve how they currently bring data and information to the marketplace and how they want to do so. The list of potential questions is never-ending, so I'll just give a few examples:

- Are we a new-content provider or are we really a repackager?

- Right now we incorporate data into our products. Might it be better to unbundle them?

- We're really good at uncovering asymmetries. Might we find a lot more if we were better data miners?

- Would internal data be salable if we improved quality?

There is only one outside-in question, and it stems directly from the "exactly the right data and information in exactly the right place . . ." mantra. It is, "What data and information needs of current (potential) customers are not met and how can we meet them?" Connecting with customers is so important that I devote the next section to the topic. But two more points regarding data and strategy are important.

First, strategy is not just a game, it is a competitive game. In formulating strategy, it is important to ask questions such as the following:

- What if our biggest competitor improves its quality?

- What if our biggest competitor develops world-class data mining capabilities?

- What if our biggest competitor figures out how to integrate its content with Other Data Company's?

The second point is that "innovation" is a strategic imperative for most organizations. If an organization wishes to fully embrace this prescription in one area, let that area be innovation. Organizations that make well-informed decisions about which innovations to pursue, craft innovation strategies and processes that are data and information ready and enabled, and listen to their customers will do just fine.

Connect Creators and Customers
of Data and Information

I've consulted on data for over twenty years now, and an important contributor to every issue I've ever worked on is that those who create data do not understand the needs of data customers. Other factors may contribute as well, but data creators not knowing what consumers expect is the easiest to solve. And connecting data and information creators and consumers is a big winner. Three of the ten habits of those with the best data—customer needs analysis, process management, and supplier management—help do just that. I discussed these topics at length in chapter 3 and appendix A, and in chapter 4 I discussed the importance of decision makers developing trusted sources.

Another way to connect data creators and customers is by shortening the feedback cycle. This is happening right now in a novel and important way in education. Individual schools report on a variety of performance indicators to districts, who in turn report to states, who in turn report to the Department of Education. The requirements of each receiving group are clearly defined (i.e., requirements are written and generally understood). Historically, however, feedback has been slow and blunt. A district might not find out that it failed to meet some requirement until the state has cut its funding. Adding insult to injury, in many cases the root cause was faulty reporting, not failure to meet the requirement per se.

As explained by Jeff Averick of Certica Solutions, who is assisting in the process, to shorten the feedback cycles, many districts and states have begun to use automated tools that check their reports against requirements before submitting them. "Everyone benefits," Averick explained. "No one, not districts nor the states, want[s] funding to be cut off by simple reporting errors. So a real source of angst is removed. Second, with data they can trust, everyone can get down to their real jobs, which is improving education."[8]

One point regarding the importance of connecting creators and customers merits further explanation here. It is that connecting those who create new data and customers is even more important for marketplace customers. This point is easiest to see for infomediators, whose entire job involves connecting creators and customers. Informationalizers must do so as well, seamlessly blending data into their products. Earlier I explained the benefits of treating regulators as customers of the new drug application process. Finally, I have already described the importance of managing data mining as an end-to-end process (chapter 6). The key need is to ensure that the data miners and those who use results are fully connected with one another.

Establish Customer-Friendly Metadata Processes

I've used the term *metadata* in several contexts in this book. Another name for metadata is *data resource data*, but either way it simply means "data about data."[9] Here I review the needs for customer-friendly metadata and recommend that organizations establish three processes that help meet the needs. The overall focus is ensuring they have "the right data" in the mantra "exactly the right data in exactly the right place . . ."

There is a subtle distinction between getting *the data right* and getting *the right data*. If someone asks me for my address and I reply "12 Maple Avenue," I may well have provided a correct datum. But if the questioner replies, "No, I meant your e-mail address," then "12 Maple Avenue" is not right. "The right data" means (again, a bit loosely) that the data provided address the needs of the (data) customer. "The right data" is a lot more involved than it may first appear. Depending on the circumstance, it may mean nothing more than a data customer easily finding the data best suited to the task at hand. My address is a good example. Easily finding what is needed is a reasonable goal. But recall that knowledge workers spend 30 percent of their time looking for needed data and over 40 percent complain that "they are bombarded with too much data."[10] The typical manager is thus overloaded with data and information but often cannot find what he or she really needs. Because new data and information are developed all the time, a certain amount of searching and bombardment is normal and healthy. But 30 percent and 40 percent, respectively, are way too high.[11]

"The right data" also implies that the data customer can easily understand what the data imply—another reasonable goal on which organizations routinely fall short. "The right data" means facilitating the work of a diverse group with a common definition of a key term. I've given several examples of organizations unable to do so. Finally, I take "the right data" to mean no data whatsoever for the hacker or thief. It only stands to reason that an organization must know where all copies of the data and information that it must protect are kept, including official copies, back-up copies, and copies on personal computers, PDAs, and other mobile devices.

Metadata therefore fall into two high-level categories:

Data about data = Where they are + What they mean

Two metadata processes aim to address these separate components head-on. The *data cataloging process* focuses on the first component, namely, where data are (including all copies), the original sources of data (where feasible), permitted and restricted uses, and how to gain access. I often liken it to the card cataloging process in a library. The *data modeling process* focuses on what data mean. It yields a data dictionary, business rules that constrain data values, and increasingly detailed data models that describe the things about which the organization has data, relationships among them, and important attributes about those things and relationships.

Organizations that have a high need for cross-departmental consensus in data definitions should also adopt a *data standards process*. I noted in the previous chapter that standards have proven remarkably difficult. Although no panacea, this process provides a repeatable means to sift through the issues, get everyone's opinion on the table, muddle though, and at least contain some brutal battles.

Importantly, the management of these metadata processes is no different from any other data-creating process. Appendix C describes in detail some of the most important features.

One company that has taken these prescriptions to heart is Aera Energy LLC.[12]

Based in Bakersfield, California, Aera consists of the onshore and off-shore exploration and production assets in California formerly operated by Shell and Mobil. Today the company is jointly owned by Shell and ExxonMobil. The company was formed in June 1997.

After he joined the company in October 1997, one of CIO David Walker's first tasks was to consolidate IT operations. In Aera's case, as in most consolidations, the most difficult step involved translating the everyday language of the business into structured data. Just as many relationship businesses struggle to define *customer*, so too in the oil business, defining a *well* (as in oil well) may be quite problematic. What exactly is a *well*?

- Is it "a hole in the ground"?

- Is it "a hole in the ground from which oil is being extracted"?

- What if, below ground level, the original hole is split into two holes, forming an inverted Y? How many wells does one have now?

- What if, through the same hole, two distinct subsurface oil zones are being produced, each one with its own production and fluid measurement equipment? How many wells does one have now?

As one of the data architecture deliverables of its enterprise architecture plan, Aera identified fifty-three "everyday language" terms (recall that such terms are usually called *entities* in data lingo) that would require careful definition. Getting the right answers was critical—even one misleading definition could affect a thousand workers every day.

Shortly after its formation, Aera overlaid a process structure, featuring eleven key processes, on top of the usual business unit structure. "Managing information" was set squarely in the middle, both feeding and depending on the other ten.

"One of our most critical decisions involved where to locate the 'manage information' process owner," observed Gene Voiland, president and CEO of Aera. "A number of people thought the position should reside in a business unit. We decided to put it in David's shop because we didn't want a line manager playing referee. This was consistent with our decision to have our CIO be responsible for information management, not just information technology management."

Walker added, "Some of my colleagues were not too keen to trust information management and data quality to an IT guy. Making our basic information technologies work well was table stakes for me."

The job of getting the right definitions was divided into two phases. The initial phase, led by Bob Palermo, enterprise architecture manager, consisted primarily of developing definitions for the initial fifty-three terms. The second phase, led by C. Lwanga Yonke, data quality manager and information management process owner, consisted of further developing these initial fifty-three terms into specific logical data models to support new applications. Palermo and Yonke, both petroleum engineers, reported directly to Walker. Throughout the two phases, specific IT expertise was provided by Marie Davis, Aera's data architect and a seasoned IT professional.

To further cement business involvement in this IT-based effort, Yonke's first step was to set up a network of thirty "stewards," who would work with each other and with their constituents to hammer out the needed definitions. These stewards were appointed by the process owners and typically were business professionals. Yonke pointed out, "It's a challenge to manage a process in which no one reports directly to you. You have to lead through influence and well-defined systems. While I was responsible for the overall process, the stewards were responsible for the individual results."

Importantly, the data modeling effort took time. Although he insisted on continual progress, Walker didn't rush things. Davis noted, "As we worked through the process, individual teams came to realize that they had to do more than just represent the interests of their own business units. They had to do what was right for everyone in Aera. That took time. It also helped us appreciate each other's perspectives and contributions a lot more."

Customer-friendly metadata is just one component of Aera's information management strategy. Aera's sustained implementation of its data quality process and enterprise architecture plan has yielded a wide array of benefits. Palermo noted, "One of our goals was to enable engineers to spend more time on engineering analysis and decision making, and less on data management. On that score we can show that we've doubled the productivity of most of these critical people." Ron John, senior vice president and head of one of Aera's business units, added, "We have also realized additional fundamental benefits. Keep in mind that deciding where to drill successful wells and deciding the best way to produce oil are inherently risky. We have taken data quality risk off the list of things we have to worry about in making these decisions. And that in itself is priceless." Adds John, "Our recent experience confirms that if a company is going to try to achieve this level of data quality for superior analysis and decision making, business units working together must partner and drive the effort."

Get in Front of Privacy and Security Issues

I reviewed the long-term complexities associated with privacy and, to a lesser degree, security in the previous chapter. That discussion notwithstanding, organizations must take near-term steps to get their arms around the issues and take prudent measures to protect themselves. They must also develop rich sensing capabilities to understand the shifting attitudes and moods of the public, the direction of legislation and regulation, their own abilities to effect policy, and the capabilities and reach of the bad guys. I see this as a highly iterative process, as outlined in figure 8-1.

The current state involves status with respect to the following.

Customers and Their Needs

1. What laws and regulations dictate what we must do?

2. What do our customers expect of us?

FIGURE 8-1

Managing privacy and security issues

The process for staying in front of privacy and security issues is highly iterative, involving understanding the current state, continuous sensing of shifting circumstances, development of new plans, and implementation.

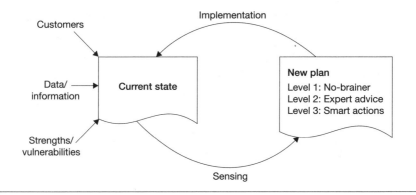

3. Who are the other stakeholders and what are their important requirements? As one example, I include employees who may wish or need to work at home or on the road in this category.

Data and Information

4. What organizational data and information might someone else want? *Note:* It is important to cast as wide a net as possible with this question. "What's in people's heads" may be just as important as computerized data.

5. What data and information are especially important? Obviously, one answer is "Data and information that the organization doesn't want others to have."

6. Where do these data and information reside? Not just in the systems and servers, but on workstations, laptops, cell phones, and other devices.

7. How do they move around? Data on the fly are more susceptible to loss or theft.

Strengths and Vulnerabilities

8. What are the possible ways that data and information could be compromised or used inappropriately?

9. Are current preventive measures effective?

10. Is the response plan in the event of a breach or violation adequate?

The new plan involves sensing that the "something new" demands further measures. Perhaps a new law has been passed, perhaps someone has discovered a new vulnerability in an operating system, or perhaps the value of a stolen identity has gone up. I like to think of potential privacy and security measures as falling into a three-layer stack, as follows:

Level 1: The "no-brainer" level

Level 2: The "experts think this is a good idea" level

Level 3: The "acting smart" level

Level 1: The "No-Brainer" Level

When I was a young manager at Bell Labs, I was uncertain how to handle a certain personnel matter. I needed to talk to someone outside the chain of command and found a particularly insightful ombudsperson. She couldn't answer my question, but she did advise me how to think it through. "Of course, it will never come to this," she said, "but imagine you're explaining what you did and why you did it to a jury. If it sounds bad, then figure out something better."

That same advice applies equally to privacy and security. If doing something—or not doing something—just sounds bad, then change your plan. This advice leads to "no-brainers," steps that all organizations must take. Here is a sampling of no-brainers:

- Follow the law.

- Don't let unencrypted laptops with sensitive data go out the door.

- Advise those who may be affected as soon as possible after a breach occurs.

- Clarify for frontline employees exactly what data and information they may and may not provide to others under common scenarios.

- Define a policy that specifies management accountabilities for privacy and security.

Level 2: The "Experts Think This Is a Good Idea" Level

Privacy and security are tough enough that most organizations require expert advice, whether in-house or contracted. Organizations need not adhere to every recommendation, but they must carefully consider each in turn. My favorite example is the recently added layer of security I have to go through to check my bank balance over the Internet. I get annoyed each time, because it adds time and trouble to my day. But experts recommend a second layer of security, particularly where identity or money might be involved.[13] My bank therefore probably made a good choice.

Level 3: The "Acting Smart" Level

If the essence of level 1 is not being stupid and the essence of level 2 is following directions, then the essence of level 3 is being smart. My best example involves selling data developed in the course of business for one purpose to other companies. There are ready markets for loan application, charitable donation, subscription, and other mailing list data. These are a nice source of revenue from data that had to be collected anyway. But many companies might be smarter to eschew the opportunity. It is better to pass up a small amount of revenue in favor of pursuing an opportunity to build trust with customers—and look smart doing so.

To look even smarter, companies can allow customers to decide whether they would like their personal data to be passed along to those who might offer useful products and services. This approach, known as *opt-in* (in contrast to *opt-out*, where customers must specifically ask that their data not be passed on), recognizes the customer as in control of his or her identity, allows those who want further offers to receive them, and saves those who do not. Customer lists screened in this manner are almost certainly more valuable. Opt-in is the norm in the European Union.

Establish a Point Person to Lead the Effort and a Data Council to Address Political Issues

A logical reaction to these prescriptions is, "Wow, this is going to be a lot of leadership and work. How would we pull it off?" In this section I propose that organizations establish a chief data officer (CDO) and a data council to formulate, lead, coordinate, and push the effort. Organizations, or departments within them, will undoubtedly start small, first naming a point person to get his or her arms around the issues and opportunities. Earlier I summarized Brent Kedzierski's role at Shell in doing just that.

The early work of Peter Serenita is also instructive. Serenita became the first CDO for JPMorgan Worldwide Securities Services in September 2006.[14] He views his job as CDO as the next logical step for a business unit that has $15.2 trillion in assets under custody.[15] "JPMorgan has always had a focus on data but the CDO role brings it to the next level. This is an evolution, not a revolution for us. JPMorgan is continually making improvements to ensure that we are providing our clients with the best data management capabilities in the industry—innovations that will keep them not only current, but ahead of the market."

Serenita views his role as being the architect and coach of the enhanced data management system. He is helping define and approve data policies, developing an efficient and cost-effective operating model, providing governance, and overseeing the convergence of technology platforms and distribution of data. He is also taking a second look at vendors to ensure strong working partnerships. "It is important to have the high-level strategy, but at the same time we need to focus on projects that are execution-ready."

Technically, Serenita has oversight authority and could add a formal "data gate" to JPMorgan's development process, but he aims to leave his mark through influence, not formal authority. Instead of managing hundreds of people, he is leveraging thousands of technologists from all data domains, across the global enterprise. There are senior-level steering committees for high-level program direction, a stakeholder group for day-to-day execution, and working groups to solve specific issues or needs. But in the end, day-in, day-out operations must deal with cost, controls, quality, and metrics.

Further, the hands-on approach helps Serenita learn as he goes. "Keep in mind," he remarked, "nobody in our industry has really done what we are focusing on now. That is, to provide quality and efficient reference data services across such a diverse set of businesses. I've got to work at the detailed level to figure out how this function should really work in order to meet the business's needs."

The potential pitfalls are many. No data management program is too small, but some can be too big, so setting the right balance is key. For effective governance, Serenita must get the right people at just the right level to the same table to make decisions. He must also resolve funding issues. All of this triggers the need for a clear connection between the program and the business problem it is solving.

Although Serenita reports to John Galante, head of technology and JPMorgan Worldwide Securities Services' CIO, he really occupies the nexus between business units, operations, and technology. "It probably doesn't matter where I report, if I'm doing my job," he explained. "Basically my job is to make connections between all three groups and provide a holistic solution across all three groups."

How to define success? One way Serenita does so is through metrics. "For the most part, we're a metrics-driven company. People focus on meeting their numbers, so if we can get the right metrics in place, the right actions will follow. Right now we're focusing on quality metrics." JPMorgan wants to demonstrate the results in additional cost reductions and efficiencies, improved business resiliency, reduction in error rates, and improved data quality.

As Kedzierski at Shell and Serenita at JPMorgan illustrate, the first jobs are to get traction and demonstrate some successes. As this happens, senior management has some very important roles to play, stemming from three interrelated observations. First, left on their own, even well-positioned and seasoned CDOs face nearly impossible challenges. The sorts of efforts that got them started will not win over the entire organization. Second, addressing the political issues of the preceding chapter and following the prescriptions of this one are not for the faint of heart. They require diligent, concerted effort. Third, ultimately senior management is responsible for the organization's governance, a responsibility it cannot delegate.

I propose a data council, comprising the organization's most senior people who are willing to help address these challenges. The council can be a new group or, preferably, new responsibilities for an existing senior leadership body, such as the operations committee. Either way, the council's job description is "to build an organization that, over time, manages data and information as professionally as it manages other assets," and in so doing to provide broad, senior support, political legitimacy, and occasional cover for the CDO, ensure that the organization's data and information program is comprehensive, well-directed, and delivering results, and that more and more people contribute.

To be effective, the data council must carry out certain functions, which, per Juran, may not be delegated.[16] First, the data council must provide visible leadership and clearly articulate the business purposes and strategy for the data and information program. This function involves no more nor less than explicit responsibility for the strategy recommendations made earlier in this chapter. Thus the data council must ensure that the quality program helps advance business strategy and that business strategy is data-enabled.

One reason that the clear articulation of strategy and business purpose is so important is that these statements help managers figure out for themselves which data and information are most important. Invariably, people need guidance that they can translate into more specific actions, such as: "Our most important data are the data that we send along to our clients. Right now they are complaining about errors. We simply must halve the number of errors clients see in the next twelve months." Thus, the owner of an order fulfillment process might conclude: "The last step in my process is invoicing, and customers complain that they are overcharged all the time. I'd better focus my efforts there."

Second, the data council must identify and support the process and supplier teams that work across departmental boundaries. It must vest these management teams with commensurate levels of accountability and authority—accountability to meet agreed-upon targets for improvement, and sufficient authority to reach them.

Third, I recommend that the council document the high-level strategy and the specific accountabilities of management in a data policy. Something as simple as the following provides both direction and empowerment:

> "Don't pass bad data on to the next person. And don't accept bad data from the previous person."[17]

Note too how such a statement fixes responsibility in the business, not IT.

The privacy and security policy recommended earlier should be part of the larger data policy. I favor simple statements that make individual responsibilities extremely clear, such as:

> "Don't take unencrypted data about our customers, suppliers, or employees from the building."

Finally, the policy may specify departmental accountabilities, such as:

> "Business unit and division heads must report on their progress on the data strategy at the end of each fiscal year."

Fourth, the data council should bear ultimate responsibility for advancing a "data culture" that helps address the thorny issues of the last chapter. Although some issues can never be completely addressed, councils can take many effective actions. For example, the process and supplier structure helps align management and data flow. The council can also clarify its expectations of IT, as discussed earlier.

Similarly, the data council can take effective action to promote data sharing, although perhaps in a slightly different guise. I know of one business unit that has at least twenty-five overlapping but disparate copies of its most important data, each supporting a fiefdom. A cost-cutting initiative might help the council reduce that number by 80 percent (a single copy is probably unrealistic and maybe even undesirable) and have the salutary effect of getting warring factions to work together.

"Advancing the data culture" involves no less than getting people, departments, and the entire organization to think and act differently. Interestingly, though, I find that most people already know that data and information matter and they wonder why senior management continues to ignore them. They are simply looking for signs that "management gets it." Part of the data council's job is thus simply to demonstrate that management does.

I now return to the CDO. Having gotten the ball rolling, the CDO's role evolves. One of the most important jobs is that of secretary to this council. I use the term *secretary* here not in the sense of an executive's secretary but of a secretary of state. A secretary of state has many varied roles: proposing strategy, recommending and implementing policy, and leading the State Department. Similarly, the CDO, as secretary of the data council, has many varied roles. Day in and day out, the CDO's job is like herding cats.

The CDO grapples with policy and implementation challenges. Thus, whereas the data council "owns" the data strategy, the data policies, and the associated business cases, the CDO actually does most of the work. This responsibility is not as straightforward as it sounds, given that data strategies and policies are difficult to define and even more difficult to implement.

To illustrate, consider the first policy statement given earlier. Should a junior analyst, citing the "Don't accept bad data" statement, refuse to complete a report because the figures provided by finance do not seem right? Or should a salesperson, citing the "Don't take unencrypted data out of the building" rule, not sign up a new customer when the encryption software on the company-issued handheld device does not work? The list of such issues can go on and on.

Convincing people that policy is even needed, advising them of their responsibilities, working out the practical details, and handling violations are all problematic. Therefore, the CDO must balance the potential utility of a policy statement against the difficulties of supporting it. There is no point in defining a policy or a strategy that cannot be supported.

The job of selling and implementing policy and strategy falls to the CDO. The CDO is the day-in, day-out face of the data program, working with the organization's various departments and process owners to help them understand their roles and obligations, integrate data into their plans, and create urgency so that the data program is given its due.[18] The CDO helps translate strategy and policy into shorter-term plans and more objective measures of success, and enlists people to join cross-departmental efforts. Finally, the CDO tracks progress by defining and assembling the data quality dashboard and helping the data council understand the results and their implications.

The CDO is also a good candidate for several day-in and day-out jobs. One is as leader of the data quality program. In this role, he or she crafts the data quality program and communicates it throughout the organization. The CDO must explain both the philosophy and the methods for managing processes and suppliers, measuring quality levels, conducting improvement activities, and so on. In this regard, one important role of the CDO is to import the techniques of data quality management and make these techniques as easy to use as possible.

For example, the seemingly simple task of renaming the Six Sigma DMAIC technique as "Our Bank's Quality Improvement Cycle" is not a straightforward exercise. The task involves selecting techniques to best suit the organization, translating them into the organization's language, and using the organization's case studies to illustrate their usage and effectiveness.

As the leader of the data quality program, the CDO either provides or arranges training and education on topics relevant to the data program, and builds deep expertise in all aspects of data and quality management so that these skills can be brought to bear on especially challenging or important issues.

The CDO is also a good candidate leader of the data supplier management program office. And I have come to believe that the chief data office may provide the best "home" for owners of the metadata processes. Although Aera is enjoying success with Yonke, who reports to IT as a process owner, he appears to be the rare exception. And the work is clearly not suited to the line. Thus, the chief data office might be the best option. Locating process owners in the CDO makes it easier to bring the organizational perspective into work on data standards.

Finally, the CDO is a good laboratory for trying out new ideas. Everything about data and information will grow and change rapidly, at least for the next generation or so. There will be new questions, opportunities, tools, methods, and risks. Where a wide perspective is required, the CDO is an excellent candidate to start the work. Kedzierski's work to bring a new generation of management reporting into Shell is an excellent example.

Keep an Open Mind Regarding Evolving the Reward Structure

It is too soon to tell whether professional management of data and information will require wholesale changes to the organization's reward system. But I can make two observations. The first is that the prescriptions offered here require people and organizations to work more closely together than most of them do now.

Of course, no reward system explicitly states, "You shouldn't share what you know with others, and we reward those who don't." But *The 48 Laws of Power* does, and many reward systems implicitly support these laws. Dennis Parton, a longtime colleague, observes that "organizations are perfectly designed to achieve the results they achieve."

Research into social networks in the work environment points to the special people whom others seek out for critical data and information, for connections, and for other insights.[19] These information brokers function much like nodes in traditional networks and are the internal infomediators.[20] They behave counter to *The 48 Laws*, supporting the free flow of data and information. They may well deserve compensation for these contributions.

Second, some people are simply better at handling data and information than others. Some can organize more, either in their heads or files; some are better at taking in tacit information; some are better at sifting the signal from the noise; some have better sources and so can acquire better data and information; some are better at drawing conclusions. The list can go on and on. Perhaps those who better handle data and information should be better compensated as well. Elliott Jacques goes further, proposing wholesale changes to the reward structure.[21] He recommends that an individual's pay grade be directly linked to the complexity of information he or she processes and the time span of the decisions that he or she makes.

Jacques may well be right. For now, organizations should keep a close eye on market forces. The demands for certain rare talents, such as data mining, continue to grow. Organizations may well need to adjust their salary structures to attract and retain certain talent.

THE BIG PICTURE

➤ An old adage advises, "It is generally considered unwise to put enough energy into your jump to get halfway across a stream." The observation is especially apt for data and information. It is easy enough to scout out the issues and opportunities, but addressing them requires real effort. Get enough of the right kinds of people involved.

➤ Avoid the "If it's in the computer it must be IT's responsibility" trap. The most important responsibilities for data and information belong in the business.

➤ Focus IT resources on automating well-defined processes.

➤ High-quality data are the linchpin for many strategies. Craft and implement a quality program to match.

➤ Couple all business strategy with data and information. Focus first on data and information–enabled innovation.

➤ Seek ways, formal and informal, to connect creators and customers of data and information.

➤ Establish customer-friendly metadata processes.

➤ Get in front of privacy and security.

➤ Establish a point person to lead the effort. Charge him or her with embracing the effort and demonstrating some successes. As the issues and opportunities clarify themselves, appoint a leader with the right title, perhaps a chief data officer.

➤ Form a data council to address political issues and build the overall management system.

CHAPTER NINE

The Next One Hundred Days

Clearly I believe that it is time for managers and organizations to explicitly recognize that data and information are business assets, to manage them as aggressively and professionally as they do other assets, and to put them to work internally and in their marketplaces. Although I expect many, perhaps even most, managers will agree with these sentiments, I also expect they will recognize the daunting challenges of doing so. Each of the tasks of systematically improving quality, bringing data and information to market, and evolving management systems requires enormous effort by itself, never mind all at once.

Nothing in this concluding chapter should give the reader any hope that there is a silver bullet, or even a clever finesse that will make the job shorter or easier. And the first step is not to craft a grand plan—most managers and organizations simply don't have the depth of understanding needed to do so. This chapter aims to help develop that depth. It outlines a one-hundred-day panorama that provides a comprehensive view of the data and information required for a selected information chain, or horizontal slice of the business. A panorama differs from a deep dive in that it strives for breadth, not depth (see "Scope of the Hundred-Day Panorama"). A financial services firm might, for

Scope of the Hundred-Day Panorama

The panorama focuses on quality, value in the eyes of the customer, and management, because these foci best elucidate why data and information must be managed as business assets and exemplify the properties discussed in chapter 1. But organizations need not limit themselves. Depending on their interests and needs, they can easily baseline (and identify opportunities) in the following additional areas:

- Effective use of data internally, especially in decision making

- Privacy and security

- Competitive position

Similarly, organizations need not feel beholden to the hundred days. The actual work described here can be completed much more quickly (by the right people), but I have allowed plenty of time for reflection.

example, select municipal bond trades for its panorama. It would then develop a deep understanding of all data and information needed for these trades, including obtaining outside data, completing the trade, and reporting ongoing profit and loss. The panorama would focus on quality, the added value customers see in the data and information provided them, management responsibilities, and politics across the chain. The panorama should include external suppliers, metadata, and clients.

The panorama aims to satisfy several objectives. Most important is to gain a real feel for data and information: their horizontal flow (I call a horizontal flow of data and information from their points of creation, their transport and transformation, and their uses by people, computers, and departments an *information chain*), how they become erroneous, how they add value, why they are such important assets, how they are managed (or not), and the distinctions between *information* and *information technology*. Participants will complete baselines and identify specific opportunities to improve quality, bring more data and information to customers, and advance governance. Although the panorama does not provide a grand plan for moving forward per se, it does help develop the knowledge needed to do so.

Overview of the Panorama Development Process

Figure 9-1 provides an overview of the process for constructing the one-hundred-day panorama. The first two steps should take a week each and are preparatory in nature. The first step aims to select an appropriate subject area, and the second to assemble a team of people across the resulting information chain.

Step 3 (weeks 3 through 5) involves determining exactly what happens across the information chain. It is a surprisingly interesting step, as the panorama team focuses on how various tasks across the organization relate to one another. Step 4 (weeks 6 through 9) provides three baselines:

- Quality

- Value in the eyes of the customer

- Management

Step 5 (weeks 10 through 12) builds on the baselines to identify opportunities for quality improvement, bringing more data and information

FIGURE 9-1

Overview of the process for developing a one-hundred-day data and information panorama

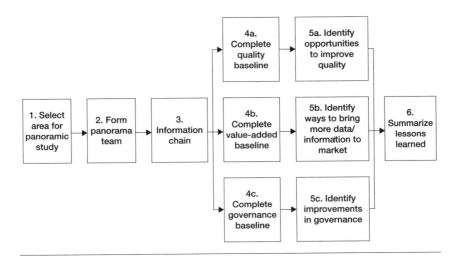

to customers, and improved management across the chain. In step 6 (weeks 13 and 14), "lessons learned" are summarized.

Week 1: Select an Area of Focus

The first step is to select a focus area. It might just as well be described as deciding what to develop a panorama of. To complete this step, senior leaders select something the organization does every day. A financial services firm might pick "conduct municipal bond trades," a shipper might choose "deliver containers," and an energy company might select "pump oil." Some judgment is required here. On the one hand, the selected area should be strategic, as trading municipal bonds is to financial institutions. On the other hand, it should not be so large that the panorama cannot be developed within one hundred days. For a hospital, "treat patients" may well prove intractable. "Deliver babies" is more manageable.

The other important part of this step is determining, at a high level, what to include in the information chain. Doing so will help identify the right team members in step 2. Ideally, the chain should extend backward into the supplier base, and forward to customers. In the financial services example, then, one such supplier provides market data (details associated with the municipal bond, prices, etc.), and one such customer is an investor.

To complete this step, create a top-line (five- to seven-box) flowchart of the selected slice. For the financial services example, such a flowchart might look something like that in figure 9-2.

FIGURE 9-2

An example of a good information chain for panoramic study

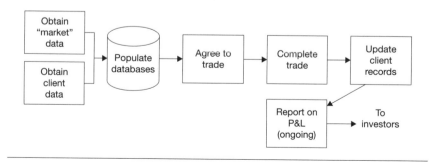

Week 2: Assemble the Panorama Development Team

The next step is to secure the services of people to help develop the panorama. Well-respected managers are good candidates. Most organizations are quite good at assembling task forces, so I will not belabor what must be done to complete this step.

Weeks 3 Through 5: Track the Flow of Data and Information

The end result of step 3 is a description and understanding of the flow of data and information across the chain. Mostly it involves a lot of back and forth. To start the step, dig into each subprocess in the flowchart of figure 9-2 to determine what data and information are needed to complete it. For example, completing a trade requires certain details about the involved parties, the municipal bond traded, the quantity, and the price.

Next, work backward to determine where each needed piece of data and information originates. There is a bit of subtlety here. For example, the trader probably *obtains* certain details about the municipal bond from a master list of securities, but the needed details do not *originate* in that master list. Rather, they are created by an outside vendor (such as Interactive Data Corporation, discussed in chapter 3) that specializes in providing such details.

This exercise continues until all the data and information needed to complete each subprocess and the original sources of those data and information have been spelled out. Importantly, it must include all data and information delivered to customers, in any form. In the trading example, clients receive trading agreements, advice, trade confirmations, and ongoing reporting of profit and loss associated with the trade. The result of the effort can be summarized in a spreadsheet like that depicted in figure 9-3.

Simplistic as figure 9-3 is, it is an eye-opener, provoking stunning reactions as managers begin to understand how their departments fit in—or not. I've heard reactions as diverse as the following:

- "I thought we were the only ones who used that data. I never understood the effect we could have on those guys one floor up."

FIGURE 9-3

Tracking the flow of data and information

Each cell of the spreadsheet lists the original source of data or information needed by a subprocess.

		Subprocess						
		Obtain market data	Obtain client data	Agree to trade	Complete trade	Update client records	Report on P&L	Data/information delivered to customers
Original source of data information	External supplier A			Bond identifier				
	External supplier B			Last trade price				
	Customer onboarding process			Customer name Account number Payment terms				
	Agree to trade			Customer agreement				
	Complete trade							Trade confirmation
	Update client records							
	Report on P&L			Payment arrangements				Monthly statement Web-based reporting

- "Why have we been doing this work all these years? Nobody cares."

- "This is much more complex than I thought. No wonder we're always fixing errors."

The last part of step 3 is to understand how data and information wind their way from the points of their creation to the points of their use. Sometimes these journeys are quite simple: data are created in one department, stored in a database, and accessed by the next. Other times, the journeys are convoluted, even circular (a sure sign of trouble). Still other times, the journeys just don't make sense. I've seen cases in which two departments thought they were working from the same data but, once the data flows were tracked, realized that in fact they used two different data sources.

A word of caution: panorama teams must resist the temptation to develop very granular flowcharts that detail each subprocess. Such deep dives may be useful in other contexts, but they miss the spirit of the panorama. Panorama teams may well find it useful to go one layer down from figure 9-2, particularly in describing how data and information wind their way around, but no deeper.

Weeks 6 Through 9: Baseline, Baseline, Baseline

The thrust of step 4 is to baseline the information chain against the practices and prescriptions herein, along three dimensions: quality, value in the eyes of customers, and management. There is a lot of work to be done here, and, as a practical matter, these baselines should be conducted in parallel, as figure 9-1 depicts.

The essence of the quality baseline is stunningly simple. It involves asking people across the organization two questions:

1. Do you have the data and information you need to do your job?

2. Are the data and information you use to do your job easy to find, accurate, and easy to understand?

Clearly, one would hope that almost everyone answers "yes" to both questions. "No" answers demand follow-up to determine what is missing, difficult to find, incorrect, or hard to understand. Look for hidden rework loops, that is, extra steps taken within subprocesses to deal with poor-quality inputs. In the financial services example, one may find that most trades are confirmed automatically. But the few plagued by bad data may require human intervention, in total the best efforts of an entire department.

It is important to include customers in the quality baseline. Subjecting members of the organization to erroneous data is bad enough, but sending those errors to customers is simply intolerable. For customers, the questions should be modified slightly, as follows:

1. Are you getting what you expect? Or are you finding errors, or data and information that are hard to understand or interpret?

2. Are you able to use the provided data and information in the ways you wish?

To complete the quality baseline, compare the management actions directed at data quality to the approach and best practices in outlined in the box "How Those with the Best Data Do It" (chapter 3). For each practice, select the most suitable response:

- We consistently adhere to best practice across the horizontal slice.

- We sometimes adhere to best practice.

- We do not adhere to best practice.

Finally, locate the overall data quality program on the data quality maturity model introduced in chapter 3 (figure 9-4).

FIGURE 9-4

The data quality maturity model

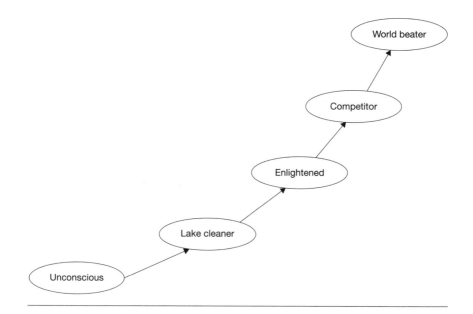

The other baselines proceed along much the same lines. For value creation, the most important questions to ask customers are as follows:

1. How do they perceive the value received?

2. What currently either stands in the way of or enhances that value?

3. [What else would they like, including new data, different formats, different means of acquiring data, better insights, and so on?] (*Note:* This question is bracketed because it is not part of the baseline per se, but will be needed in the next step.)

The answers can be fascinating. In the trading example, one might assume that the greatest value lies in the advice about the trade (provided, say, in the "agree on trade" subprocess). But many clients are their own advisers. They may appreciate ongoing reporting of the profit and loss associated with the trade even more.

The third, and usually most interesting, baseline involves management. To complete this baseline, determine, as comprehensively as possible, exactly who is responsible for each piece of data and information everywhere along the chain, both inside subprocesses and between them. The simplest way to do so is to ask managers the following questions:

1. What data and information are they personally responsible for?

2. Who is responsible for the data and information they need to do their job?

3. What are their responsibilities to the next person in line?

Impose very high standards here—do not assume a manager is responsible unless he or she agrees that this is the case. And find out what "being responsible" means to each manager. Are there policy documents that spell out responsibility? Are the handoffs from one manager or department to the next clear? Does some sort of information chain management team have end-to-end accountability? Be on the lookout for situations in which two departments each think the other is responsible, especially line organizations and the IT department. Find out who, exactly, is responsible for the external data and information received from external vendors and delivered to customers.

To complete this baseline, also review the list of social issues in the box "Twelve Barriers to Effective Management of Data and Information Assets" (chapter 7). Remember that "all politics is local," so describe the issues uncovered in some detail.

In conducting these baselines, the panorama team should keep a special eye on scope. For example, if managers, traders, or clients, respectively, make the following remarks, the panorama team may wish to expand the scope, in effect redrawing figure 9-2:

- "I think we do okay in our actual work, but I don't have the reports I need to know for sure."

- "You know, I don't really have much trouble with trading. But I do have trouble with my commissions."

- "You didn't ask me about them, but I get a lot of incorrect 1099s every year. And I have to redo my taxes."

Weeks 10 Through 12: Opportunities, Opportunities, Opportunities

Follow up the baseline by developing detailed lists of opportunities to improve quality, to bring more data and information to market, and to advance the management system. Think both near and long term. For example, a number of people may cite anecdotes in which erroneous data caused them great concern. But absent a measurement, it is impossible to separate the one-time anecdotes from the chronic problems that occur everyday. Thus, a short-term measurement involving one hundred trades might shed considerable light on the true situation. A midterm improvement might involve developing a series of requirements documents that illuminate for all sources how the data they create affect those downstream. A longer-term improvement might involve implementing a vendor management program.

I find the lists of opportunities to bring more data and information to customers the most interesting result of the exercise. I recently facilitated a session between one company and ten of its customers that yielded seventy-five ideas for enhancing current information products.

Customers (especially the leading-edge ones) almost always have dozens of creative ideas, essentially free for the asking.

Developing a list of ways to advance the management system is difficult, primarily because cultural change takes time. Still, it is critical that the panorama team spend time thinking through the opportunities. It can use the twelve social issues of chapter 7 and the governance recommendations of chapter 8 as checklists. The following examples illustrate the depth of thinking required here.

Most panorama teams will, for example, identify "siloed departments and technologies" as the critical factor that impedes the easy flow of data and information. They may be tempted to propose a new enterprise system as a solution, but the panorama team must think much more deeply. Are siloed departments the *cause* or the *result* of siloed technologies? In many companies, departments were siloed long before the advent of computers, so the proposed enterprise system will not address the root issue. I've proposed big-P process management as the means to manage the flow of data and information across siloed departments, but it is no panacea. The panorama team must think through how that might work, what people must be involved, and how process and functional management will work together.

As a second example, the panorama team should think through the implications of a potential data czar. It should scope out what the role would entail, identify potential candidates, and consider reporting options. It should look at the current management across the chain: who would help the czar succeed, who would sit on the sidelines, and who would get in the way?

Weeks 13 and 14: "So What Did We Really Learn?"

Another way of viewing the one-hundred-day panorama is that it provides a structured approach to wallowing around in data and information. Up to now, the panorama has taken its participants into the muck and the mire, with a focus on the business-directed prescriptions of this book. For the final two weeks the team should pick its collective head up and ask "What did we really learn about data and information?" I offer the following questions as starting points:

- Are data and information really business assets across this information chain? If so, in what respects? If not, why not?

- Which of the properties discussed in chapter 1 are most critical for understanding this chain?

- What are the long-term implications?

The panorama team should not expect to fully appreciate everything there is to know about data and information in one hundred days. Indeed, I've had the great privilege and pleasure of wallowing around in data and information, with many great companies, for thirty years. I'm continually impressed by how little I really understand. But the team should strive to summarize its ruminations in a half-dozen or so key points. Many, such as "Data and information create value as they move around. And we're not managing that movement at all," will appear obvious in retrospect. But it is these "Ahas!" that organizations must take to heart as they develop programs to manage and leverage their data and information assets.

THE BIG PICTURE

➤ These are exciting times for managers and organizations that embrace data and information. They're creating a new future for themselves, their organizations, and their industries.

➤ Unless you have already done so, there is no time like the present to unravel the mysteries of data and information. Jump in, striving for breadth—from suppliers through departments to customers.

APPENDIX A

The Ascent of Process

People have been defining and improving work processes forever. To my knowledge, the first to make a scientific study of work processes was Frederick Taylor, with his famous time and motion studies. Taylor focused on individual work processes as simple as unloading a boxcar and consistently showed how to make enormous improvements.[1] The impact of Taylor's work was and is far ranging, with implications from pay scales to management attitude. In terms of my spectrum from little-p to big-P, Taylor's primary focus was on the little-p processes. This is extremely important—few can successfully concentrate on the big-P when constituent little-p's do not perform at least tolerably well.

Two of the first big-P insights came from Samuel Colt and Henry Ford. Colt recognized that interchangeable parts could simplify gun manufacture and make the weapons easier to maintain in the field.[2] Interchangeable parts, quite obviously, must be exactly alike, what we now call decreased variation. Interchangeable parts meant that each gun was no longer handcrafted but assembled, reducing the time it took to make one and increasing manufacturing capacity. Henry Ford introduced the notion of an assembly line, arranging the steps in building an automobile along a giant moving line of vehicles, replacing the various crafts along the way with simpler, better-defined little-p process steps.[3]

Four other names bear mention. First is Walter Shewhart, who developed the control chart.[4] Control charts, a handy invention that has proven its worth in millions of settings, make it possible to systematically understand manufacturing variation, recognize process capabilities, and take appropriate actions "in process." A little-p process can be brought back into control before it affects a downstream process, and processes can be more systematically improved.

Joseph Juran and W. Edwards Deming built on these ideas. Juran is best known for the so-called Juran trilogy, which combined the notions of quality planning (determining customer needs), quality control, and quality improvement.[5] Deming recognized the importance of applying these concepts not just to manufacturing but also to other processes and, indeed, to management itself.[6] More recently, Michael Hammer introduced the concept of reengineering, an approach aimed at large-scale improvement of big-P processes.[7] Too many existing processes have outgrown their Industrial Age roots and must be wholly reexamined—from real customer needs to methods of completing and managing the work to relationships with suppliers.

Literally millions of others have contributed to making manufacturing processes more effective and efficient—and so hastened the full flower of the Industrial Age. In the last twenty years or so, increasing attention has been paid to service and so-called knowledge processes. Some speculate that it will be difficult to impose the discipline that processes require on knowledge workers.[8] This is undoubtedly true. It was not easy to get craftsmen to give up their crafts in favor of assembly line work, even if it did offer better pay. And study of failed enterprise systems suggests that knowledge workers do not readily accept the prepackaged processes that come with these systems. Thus, it may take some time before little-p processes are optimized.

I think that the bigger opportunity lies in big-P processes, however. Almost all people and departments are doing the best job they can, to the limits of their training, tools, and knowledge of what is expected. Within those limits, most really are doing a pretty good job. But if they (both people and departments) do not understand who their customers are and what those customers need, how their work affects them, where they fit in the process, and what they should expect from their suppliers, then one should expect simple problems to go undetected and have enormous impact. Almost all people and departments are more than happy to accommodate others—when they understand the bigger picture.

Hence the beauty of big-P process: day in and day out, people still work within their little-p processes, but they know where they fit, who their customers are, and how an error downstream hurts everyone. Big-P process makes it easier to establish the requirements and feedback channels with the "next person in line," "the person after him," "the person just before," and "the person before him." It forces the root causes into the open, where people can deal with them in a less politically charged setting.

This point is especially pertinent to data and information, which can cross any number of departmental barriers as they flow across the organization. Unless that end-to-end flow is actively managed, data errors are almost certain to be created in one department and have an impact far downstream. Big-P process management works because it aligns the little-p and middle-p processes owned by these departments in the direction of the customer and makes it clear where each smaller process fits.

Information Technology's Support for Data and Information

The information technology (IT) department's first and most important role is to provide (make or buy, customize, implement, and support) applications to help business processes perform faster, more economically, and with greater capacity. These applications must do the following:

- Ensure that people can access the data they need and understand them ("the right data in the right place, at the right time, and in the right format" portion of our goal)

- Help those who use them create correct data for later data customers

Both points require that applications be tightly aligned with business processes and that the business processes themselves be well defined. Many business processes do not meet that standard, and one of the toughest jobs for IT managers is advising their business counterparts that this is the case (see "Repairing the Damage").

IT must also build into its applications the tools needed to create high-quality data. Particularly exciting tools include the following:

- Editing capabilities that help people correct their own mistakes

- Measurement capabilities to help process and supplier teams know how well customer needs are being met and to identify ways to improve the process

- Utilities that help users quickly and easily learn data definitions

- Workflow capabilities that manage the movement of work from one group to the next, track cycle time, and track exceptions

Second, IT is responsible for the technical infrastructure, including the organization's databases, needed hardware and software, and the communications infrastructure. This technical infrastructure becomes, in effect, the foundation on which the applications described earlier reside. Database administrators, who tune databases for optimal performance, thus belong in IT.

Repairing the Damage

Many ITers bemoan the fact that they have not yet been viewed as strategic partners with their business counterparts. I have conducted no serious survey, but most people on the business side have a very dim view of IT. They view ITers as arrogant, disconnected, and generally unresponsive. Under these circumstances, it is premature for IT to even consider being viewed as a strategic partner.

My analysis suggests a powerful first step. Process owners should view IT as a supplier and manage it just like any other external supplier. Conversely, IT should treat process owners as customers and strive to become a trusted supplier. Only then should IT talk of becoming a strategic partner.

Third, much of the job of implementing security and privacy policies falls to IT. The task is simultaneously daunting, thankless, and essential. Here too IT is in a tricky spot. It is easy to conclude that IT bears principal responsibility for privacy and security. However, interpreting the body of new law is far beyond its expertise, and many breaches are far more mundane. Furthermore, hackers are ingenious and the chances of catching them are quite low. Conversely, legitimate customers want faster, easier access through more devices. PDAs are but the most current example.

A fourth task for IT is implementing data cleanups, meaning finding and fixing erroneous data, changing formats, adding new fields, and so on. Of course, data cleanups are a task of last resort, but sometimes new customer needs require them. The task is best led by IT.

Organizations should not conduct data cleanups unless the processes creating new data are of high quality (there are rare exceptions to this rule). Some people, however, argue for immediate cleanups and fixing the process later. The trap is that the cleanup addresses the immediate problem without resolving the underlying issues. When this occurs, subsequent cleanups are inevitable. Thus, this prescription calls for IT to lead *one-time cleanups only*.

IT's fifth and most complex role involves innovation. Innovation comes in many forms and on many levels. On one level, new technologies enable new process designs. The Internet is a great example. Companies can exploit it in processes to enroll customers, to sell many products and services, to help customers solve their own problems, and in thousands of other ways. Similarly, enterprise systems can provide new process designs. By keeping abreast of new technologies, IT departments advise process management teams of new ways to design their processes.

This role also extends to "breakthrough technologies," those that seemingly have the potential to change everything. Hype aside, breakthrough technologies don't come along very often. Further, most don't come to full flower until the business processes to leverage these technologies are worked out. Indeed, their value derives not from the technologies themselves but from the business processes they enable.

To contribute effectively, IT departments must display both judgment and timing—judgment to select the new technologies (breakthrough or otherwise) that are most likely to benefit the organization, and timing to advise process managers at the right time. Too soon and they will spin their wheels. Too late and they will lose opportunity.

Note that this role stops short of telling process owners how to design their processes. It merely involves keeping them fully advised of their options. Some IT departments should go further, maintaining "process laboratories" that help process managers test potential changes.[1] In its usual sense, a *laboratory* is "a place providing opportunity for experimentation, observation, or practice in a field of study."[2] Process laboratories are set up specifically for experimenting with processes. In the foreground, they allow people to test new ways of completing tasks, features, computer screens, and process management tools. In the background, they employ simulations to evaluate end-to-end process performance for thousands of options.

With these two features, process managers need not "trust us [in IT]—your people will love the new system." They can send people to the lab, give them hands-on experience, and ask them what they think. Nor must they simply wait and see what a potential improvement yields. They can go to the lab, mock it up, run a trial, and get definitive results. Nor must they simply guess how many new people will be required if volume doubles. They can run an experiment and get a much better answer.

Metadata Processes

As discussed in chapter 2, metadata are data about the data, and metadata processes are those processes through which metadata are developed and kept current. Whereas most managers are very familiar with their department's operational and decision-making processes, they've less experience with the metadata processes. Thus, this appendix provides an overview of the three metadata processes recommended in this book.

The Data Cataloging Process: Keeping Track of Your Data

I almost always find the customer–supplier model (recall figure 3-1) an excellent tool for providing a high-level overview of a process. I like to work from right to left, starting with customers and their needs. Customers of the data cataloging process include business process owners, browsers (those looking around for something they cannot fully define), and those charged with protecting security. Their needs are something like the following (table C-1):

TABLE C-1

Customers and needs of the data cataloging process

Data catalog customer	Need(s)
Business process owners	Find potential data suppliers
Browsers	Learn what data the organization has and where they may be obtained
Security officials	Keep track of where all data reside and who is permitted access

The data catalog gets its name from the good, old-fashioned card catalog at the local library. Three important features in the latter are the Dewey Decimal System (DDS), the International Standard Book Number (ISBN), and interlibrary loans. In the card catalog process, the On-Line Computer Library System assigns a classification number based on the DDS. When a local library obtains the book, it thus knows where to place it in its stacks. The library creates one or more "cards," summarizing all the pertinent data, which it files in its card catalog. (Readers older than about twenty will recall the long, skinny files they used to search to find the books they needed.) One item on the card is the book's ISBN, a ten-digit number that uniquely identifies the book. Given ISBNs and interlibrary loans, even the smallest local library can obtain books for its patrons from around the world. It is a simple, effective system that has served the needs of library patrons for generations and has gotten even better with the advent of online, interconnected catalogs.

In principle, the data cataloging process works in much the same way. There are complications, however. There are two important reasons that the card catalog process works. First, publishers and libraries themselves are strongly motivated to share. Although the process aims to serve library patrons, both publishers and libraries also benefit. Second, the DDS and ISBN standards help make it (relatively) easy to share.

As discussed in chapter 7, not all people want to share data, even when it technically belongs to their organization rather than themselves. Second, the data cataloging process must extend to all physical copies. Although libraries certainly do not encourage patrons to copy books, they make no attempt to keep track of any copies that are made.

Organizations cannot afford that luxury for their data. To be effective, the data cataloging process must keep track of all copies, be they on mainframes, laptops, tape backups, or paper.

Further, since most important data are electronic, the ease with which they can be copied onto smaller and smaller devices that are themselves valuable exacerbates the problem (it is tough to copy a book—the first time, anyway!). For example, correspondents on the NBC Nightly News described Afghan merchants selling flash drives (small data storage devices that plug into the USB ports on personal computers) containing classified data in a bazaar just outside a U.S. military base.[1] Evidently civilian employees had stolen the flash drives and sold them to the merchants, who were simply reselling the hardware—there was no evidence presented of any plot to steal and sell classified data and information (presumably such a sale would not have taken place in the bazaar).

It follows that effective data cataloging processes must address these issues. Strong policies that advise people when and to where they may copy data and of their obligations to report on the copies they make are essential. An effective data cataloging process must also:

- Make it easy to follow the policy

- Make the policy difficult to violate

- Provide sufficient enforcement so that violations can be detected and rectified quickly

---

The Data Modeling Process: Capturing the Right Attributes About the Right Things

Ultimately, the world is very complex, and people and organizations employ models to simplify things. All sorts of models exist: clay models, mathematical models, and computer models, to name just a few. A data model consists of data and specifies the things of interest to an organization, calls out important attributes of those things, describes interrelationships among them, specifies the layout of data in the computer, and provides a data dictionary.[2]

People have, of course, laid out data in columns and rows since antiquity. But it is only recently that we have needed a fancy term, *data model,* to describe these work products. The reason is computers. In the early days of computers, storage space was expensive, so programmers had to be clever about what data were stored. Later needs for fast access imposed further requirements on data storage. In the last decade or so, the need to get department-sized systems to talk to each other has become more and more important.

Not surprisingly, there are many customers of data models, and their needs are diverse (table C-2):

TABLE C-2

Customers and needs of the data modeling process

Data modeling customer	Need(s)
Data customers—people who use data to complete operations, satisfy a customer, or make a decision	Understand what the various data elements mean
Systems planners and analysts responsible for developing and extending databases	Complete list of entities and attribute keys
Technicians who provide and optimize physical storage and access	Deep technical details

Because the number of customers for and uses of data models are so great, many organizations employ not one but three data models: conceptual, logical, and physical. Dave Hay's definitions of these models are both simple and powerful, so I repeat them here in full:[3]

- "The conceptual model describes the fundamental nature of the business, without regard to how business information might be stored." Hay calls this the "architect's view."

  Although I agree with Hay's definition, I think a conceptual model is much more than the architect's view, because the fundamental nature of an organization is everyone's concern.

- "The logical model is a representation of that information as organized for a particular data management technology." Hay calls this the "designer's view." A description of the rows and columns of a spreadsheet (paper or Excel) is an example.

- "The physical model describes how data might be stored in a physical medium." Hay calls this the "builder's view."

One interesting feature of the data modeling process is that customers are also its most important suppliers. Their input is essential if data modelers are to understand what the words people use every day mean in the context of their work, those fundamental things needed to complete work, the needed attributes, and so forth.

Several factors conspire to make data modeling an especially difficult process to manage. First is the range of customers and their needs. Here the animosity between IT (which frequently creates the data models) and the business has serious repercussions. Both should share blame. Too often data modelers are only interested in their systems, and the needs of business customers are relegated to a second tier. For their part, modelers may complain that business process owners do not give them the time they need to learn what they need to know to model effectively.

Similarly, the diversity of work products complicates data modeling. Physical data models are detailed and technical, whereas conceptual models are presented as abstract pictures that are hard to understand and value. Harried businesspeople conclude that the only tangible output is a working database, so they wonder why conceptual and logical models are needed at all (see "Enterprise Architecture"). This in turn leads them to conclude that data modeling is an esoteric, technical process that belongs in IT. A vicious cycle arises that is difficult to thwart.

A final complication is the range of work. Conceptual data modeling is quite abstract. A few people have the knack of interacting with business process owners and producing elegant, even beautiful models. (Most, unfortunately, produce conceptual models that are far too complex and mechanical.) In contrast, the work of optimizing a data structure is quite technical.

Enterprise Architecture

In the late 1980s and early 1990s, so-called enterprise architectures enjoyed popularity with some companies. These well-meaning projects often used the Zachman framework in an attempt to connect every data element, process, and computer system to their business purpose or purposes. The enterprise architectures never got very far, however. They took too long and didn't provide near-term paybacks along the way. This experience may contribute to senior management's unease with data modeling, which is too bad. Some of the concepts in the Zachman framework are still ahead of their time. And a deep, fundamental understanding of an organization's most important "things" and the relationships among them can only pay dividends—in many ways!

The Data Standards Process:
Getting People on the Same Page

A *standard* is "something established by authority, custom, or general consent as a model or example."[4] In most industries, standards have proven their worth time and again. As described in chapter 7 there are a few data standards, including the aforementioned ISBN, Universal Product Codes (UPC), and codes for identifying equities (CUSIPs). Still, most organizations, large ones anyway, are bedeviled by the lack of standards for key data items such as CUSTOMER, PRODUCT, and SALE.

I've already noted that problems arise when the organization must answer questions such as "Did we get a market share bump in the latest campaign?" or "How many customers do we have?" Such questions require input from two or more departments, each defining the terms slightly differently. The only solution is standards, at least for cross-departmental work.

It follows that anyone who needs to work across department lines is a potential customer of the data standards process. The typical needs of three customer groups are listed below (table C-3):

TABLE C-3

Customers and needs of the data standards process

Data standards customer	Need(s)
Senior leadership	Get everyone on the same page
Corporate	Answer questions that require inputs from two or more departments
Cross-unit marketing	Assemble a total view of the customer

It is difficult to get started on data standards. Most people acknowledge that they are important, but it is difficult to put in the needed effort until there is a crisis. At that point, the standard operating procedure is to form a task force, lock people from across the organization in a room, and instruct them to hammer out a solution. It is difficult, demanding work, and the results are usually unsatisfactory. The task force takes a long time (sometimes so long that an ad hoc solution to the original crisis obviates the task force), the proposed solutions are too grandiose, and there is no way to administer them.

A better way is the process adopted by recognized standards bodies, such as the American National Standards Institute (ANSI) and the International Standards Organization (ISO). Important features include the following:

- Solid efforts, early on, to involve anyone who might wish to contribute to the standard

- A voting mechanism whereby a proposed standard is either accepted, rejected, or returned for further work

- A means of obtaining an exception

- A means to promulgate and enforce the standard

Notes

Introduction

1. Thomas H. Davenport and Jeanne G. Harris, *Competing on Analytics: The New Science of Winning* (Boston: Harvard Business School Press, 2007).

2. Stewart Taggart, "The 20-Ton Packet," Wired.com, October 1999, http://www.wired.com/wired/archive/7.10/ports.html.

3. Privacy Rights Clearinghouse, "A Chronology of Data Breaches Reported Since the ChoicePoint Incident," http://www.privacyrights.org/ar/ChronDataBreaches.htm.

4. Nicholas Carr, "IT Doesn't Matter," *Harvard Business Review*, May 2003, 41–49.

5. Carr does not use this model. He calls the first phase "IT build-out," although I prefer "coherent IT infrastructure," after *Understanding Information,* report by P-E Center for Management Research, Surrey, UK, 1994. *Understanding Information* aimed to help IT departments sort out "the contradiction between the evident importance of information and our ignorance of what it is and how it should be managed." It is a forerunner to this model.

Chapter 1

1. Nicholas Carr, "IT Doesn't Matter," *Harvard Business Review*, May 2003, 41–49.

2. Rick Whiting, "Hamstrung by Defective Data," *Information Week*, May 8, 2006, http://www.informationweek.com/story/showArticle.jhtml?articleID=187200771.

3. Lou Gerstner, quoted in P. McDougall, "More Work Ahead," *Information Week*, December 18–25, 2000, 22.

4. Henry Petroski, *Invention by Design* (Cambridge, MA: Harvard University Press, 1996).

5. Defining information based on the reduction of uncertainty, such as occurs in this test scenario, has a rich tradition. Claude Shannon of Bell Labs first introduced the notion for communications. Shannon even developed a measure for the quantity of information, based on how much the uncertainty was reduced. Bayesian statisticians also use this concept. See C. E. Shannon, "A Mathematical Theory of Communication," *Bell System Technical Journal* 27 (July 1948): 379–423 and *Bell System Technical Journal* 27 (October 1948): 623–656.

6. Jeff McMillan, personal communication, November 6, 2007.

7. See John Seely Brown and Paul Duguid, *The Social Life of Information* (Cambridge, MA: Harvard Business School Press, 2002), for other life histories of data and information.

8. Roger Clarke, "Information Wants to Be Free," http://www.anu.edu.au /people/Roger.Clarke/II/IWtbF.html. Clarke claims that Brand first made the comment at the first Hacker's Conference, in 1984.

9. McMillan.

Chapter 2

1. Dean Foust and Aaron Pressman, "Credit Scores Not-So-Magic Numbers," *BusinessWeek*, February 18, 2008, 33.

2. Roben Farzad, "Let the Blame Game Begin," *BusinessWeek*, July 27, 2007.

3. Gretchen Morgenson, "Foreclosures by Lender Investigated," *New York Times*, November 11, 2007.

4. See, for example, "Postcards from the Ledge," *The Economist,* December 22, 2007, 9.

5. Hundreds of articles have already been written on this topic, and there will be many more to come. This summary is as of December 10, 2007, and makes use of Greg Ip, Mark Whitehouse, and Aaron Luchetti, "US Mortgage Crisis Rivals S&L Meltdown," The Wall Street Journal Online, December 10, 2007, http://online.wsj .com/article_print/SB119724657737318810.html, and "2007 Subprime Mortgage Financial Crisis," Wikipedia, http//en.wikipedia.org/, as of December 10, 2007.

6. Paul Krugman, "A Crisis of Faith," *New York Times*, February 15, 2008.

7. See for example, Gretchen Morgensen, "O Wise Bank, What Do We Do? (No Fibbing Now)," *New York Times*, Week in Review, January 27, 2008.

8. As I better understood the connection between "the news" and bad data, I started cutting out newspaper articles in the mid-1990s. I have amassed well over five thousand since then. The accounts presented here are culled from that collection.

9. Those interested in reliving the tense days after the 2000 election will enjoy *36 Days: The Complete Chronicles of the 2000 Presidential Election Crisis* (New York: Times Books, 2001), by correspondents of the *New York Times*. In reading through it, notice the tight linkage between virtually every legal challenge and some data issue.

10. Katherine Q. Sleelye, "Study Says 2000 Election Missed Millions of Votes," *New York Times*, July 17, 2001.

11. David Postman, "Rossi Will Not Appeal Election Ruling," *Seattle Times*, June 6, 2005.

12. "Orbiter Lost Because NASA Forgot Metrics," *Asbury Park Press*, October 1, 1999.

13. Bill Brannon, "Key Findings of Investigation into BRAC Decision to Close Fort," APP.com, December 9, 2007, http://www.app.com/apps/pbcs.dll/article?AID=2007712090422&template=printart.

14. Martin Fackler, "Error Disrupts Bond Trading in Japan," NYTimes.com, June 30, 2006, http://www.nytimes.com/2006/06/30/business/worldbusiness/30yen.html.

15. Karen W. Arenson and Alan Finder, "Technical Problems Cause Errors in SAT Test Scores," NYTimes.com, March 8, 2006, http://www.nytimes.com/2006/03/08/education/08sat.html.

16. Randal C. Archibold, "Girl in Transplant Mix-up Dies After Two Weeks," NYTimes.com, February 23, 2003, http://query.nytimes.com/gst/fullpage.html?res=9C07E2D7113DF930A15751C0A9659C8B63&scp=1&sq=girl+in+transplant+mix-up&st=nyt.

17. Kim Nash and Deborah Gage, "We Really Did Screw Up," *Baseline*, May 2007.

18. Privacy Rights Clearinghouse, "A Chronology of Data Breaches Reported Since the ChoicePoint Incident," http://www.privacyrights.org/ar/ChronDataBreaches.htm.

19. "Lost in the Post," *The Economist*, November 24, 2007, 14.

20. Penelope Patsuris, "The Corporate Scandal Sheet," Forbes.com, August 26, 2002, http://www.forbes.com/2002/07/25/accountingtracker_print.html.

21. Huron Consulting Group, *2004 Annual Review of Financial Reporting Matters* (Chicago: Huron Consulting Services, 2005).

22. Sam Roberts, "Census Shows Slight Dip in City, But Demographers Beg to Differ," NYTimes.com, March 16, 2006, http://www.nytimes.com/2006/03/16/nyregion/16census.html.

23. George Tenet, "DCI Statement on the Belgrade Chinese Embassy Bombing," July 22, 1999, http://web.archive.org/web/20010414083545/www.usconsulate.org.hk/uscn/others/1999/0722d.htm.

24. Mark Mazzetti, "US Finding Says Iran Halted Nuclear Arms Effort in 2003," *New York Times*, December 4, 2007.

25. See, for example, Susan Feldman and Chris Sherman, *The High Cost of Not Finding Information* (Framingham, MA: IDCX, 2001); and *LexisNexis Workplace Productivity Study,* 2008, www.lexisnexis.com/literature.pdf/Workplace_Productivity_Survey_Results.

26. See also Susan Feldman, "The High Cost of Not Finding Information," *KMWorld* 13, no. 3 (March 2004), http://www.kmworld.com/Articles/Editorial /Feature/The-high-cost-of-not-finding-information-9534.aspx.

27. As reported in Marianne Kolbasuk McKee, "The Useless Hunt for Data," *Information Week*, January 1/8, 2007, 19.

28. This figure is taken from the Gartner study cited in Rick Whiting, "Hamstrung by Defective Data," *Information Week*, May 8, 2006, http://www .informationweek.com/story/showArticle.jhtml?articleID=187200771. It agrees with detailed measurement made in a variety of setting by the author's clients.

29. My support for this claim will not pass scientific scrutiny. Some years ago I began making the claim in talks as something of a lightning rod. People come up to me afterward from time to time to tell me that my estimate is far too low—for their organization, anyway.

30. Dennis Overbye, "Vote Makes It Official: Pluto Isn't What It Used to Be," NYTimes,com, August 25, 2006, http://www.nytimes.com/2006/08/25/science /space/25pluto.html

31. Lisa Myers, "Stolen Military Data Is for Sale in Afghanistan," MSNBC .com, April 13, 2006, http://www.msnbc.msn.com/id/12305580/.

32. Wayne Eckerson, *Data Quality and the Bottom Line: Achieving Business Success Through a Commitment to High Quality Data* (Seattle, WA: The Data Warehousing Institute Report Series, 2002).

33. Edward McNicholas, partner in the law firm of Sidley Austin, as quoted in Michael Friedenberg, "The Coming Epidemic," *CIO* magazine, May 15, 2006, 14.

34. T. Friedman, "Data Quality 'Firewall' Enhances Value of the Data Warehouse," Gartner Research, April 13, 2003, and "CRM Demands Data Cleansing," Gartner Research, December 3, 2004.

35. I, like many others, have benefited from a long-time association with Dr. Godfrey. His insights into both the methods of quality management and "where it fits" have proven stunningly accurate over a long period of time.

Chapter 3

1. Joseph M. Juran and A. Blanton Godfrey, *Juran's Quality Handbook*, 5th ed. (New York: McGraw-Hill, 1998).

2. Michael Treacy and Fred Wiersema, *The Discipline of Market Leaders: Choose Your Customers, Narrow Your Focus, Dominate Your Market* (Reading, MA: Addison-Wesley, 1995).

3. This hierarchy of data needs would not pass scientific scrutiny, but it is not intended to. Rather, it aims to help the reader gain a better perspective on data and information. Note that these needs correspond to the first five critical data quality problems cited in chapter 2.

4. Interactive Data was a supplier to one of my clients. This case study was developed via a series of conversations in 2007. Interactive Data has approved this write-up.

5. This quotation is from David A. Garvin, "The Processes of Organization and Management," *Sloan Management Review* (Summer 1998): 33–50.

6. AT&T Quality Steering Committee, *Process Quality Management and Improvement Guidelines* 1.1, AT&T Quality Steering Committee, 1998.

7. Jeffrey K. Liker, *The Toyota Way: 14 Management Principles from the World's Greatest Manufacturer* (New York: McGraw-Hill, 2004).

8. Thomas C. Redman, "Improve Data Quality for Competitive Advantage," *Sloan Management Review* (Winter 1995): 99–107.

9. For a financial services example, see John Fleming, "Creating a Supplier Management Program That Utilizes Total Quality Management at the Data Source" (address to FIMA 06 Conference, New York, NY, March 14, 2006).

10. I believe my long-time colleague, Bob Pautke, first coined the term *accurometer*.

11. Thomas C. Redman, "Measuring Data Accuracy: A Framework and Review," in *Information Quality*, eds. Richard Y. Wang, Elizabeth M. Pierce, Stuart E. Madnick, and Craig W. Fisher (Armonk, NY: M.E. Sharpe, 2005).

12. After Joseph M. Juran, *Managerial Breakthrough* (New York: McGraw-Hill, 1964), 183–188.

13. Tele-Tech Services was one of my clients. This case study was developed via a series of conversations in 2007. Tele-Tech has approved this write-up.

14. Mikel Harry and Richard Schroeder, *Six Sigma: The Breakthrough Management Strategy Revolutionizing the World's Top Corporations* (New York: Doubleday, 2000).

15. Joseph M. Juran, *Juran on Leadership for Quality: An Executive Handbook* (New York: Free Press, 1989).

16. Actually, this statement is not correct. Organizations thought a lot about managing and maintaining paper records. The difficulties and expense of doing so were primary motivations for adopting computers. See Thomas K. Landauer, *The Trouble with Computers* (Cambridge, MA: MIT Press, 1995), 247.

17. Joseph M. Juran, "Made in USA: A Renaissance in Quality," *Harvard Business Review*, July–August 1993, 47.

18. Morningstar was a supplier to one of my clients. This case study was developed via a series of conversations in 2007. Morningstar has approved this write-up.

19. My favorite description of change management is John P. Kotter, *Leading Change* (Boston: Harvard Business School Press, 1996).

20. Peter Aiken, M. David Allen, Burt Parker, and Angela Mattia, "Measuring Data Management Practice Maturity: A Community's Self-Assessment," *Computer*, April 2007, 48–56.

21. There is an important potential for bias in this analysis. A level 1 organization (data unconscious) might be less likely to respond to Aiken's survey request and is certainly less likely to show up in my consulting practice. Thus, such organizations may be undercounted. Although I have no way to reliably estimate the impact of this bias, I do not think it is central to the main points here.

Chapter 4

1. I strongly recommend the January 2006 special issue of *Harvard Business Review* devoted to decision making.

2. Dick Martin, *Tough Calls: AT&T and the Hard Lessons Learned from the Telecom War* (New York: Amacom, 2005).

3. CFO Research Services with Deloitte Consulting, *IQ Matters: Senior Finance and IT Executives Seek to Boost Information Quality* (Boston: CFO Publishing, 2005).

4. Peter M. Drucker, "Be Data Literate—Know What to Know," *Wall Street Journal*, December 1, 1992, 98–107.

5. W. Edwards Deming, *Quality, Productivity, and Competitive Position* (Cambridge: MIT Center for Advanced Engineering Study, 1982), 248.

6. Martin, *Tough Calls*.

7. Thomas H. Davenport, "Competing on Analytics," *Harvard Business Review,* January 2006.

8. Michael Moss, "Mammogram Team Learns from Its Errors," *New York Times*, June 28, 2002, http://query.nytimes.com/gst/fullpage.html?sec=health&res=9903EED7133EF93BA15755C0A9649C8B63.

9. Battles are studied extensively not just by the military but by reporters and historians, often hundreds of years afterward. See David Zucchino, *Thunder Run: The Armored Strike to Capture Baghdad* (New York: Atlantic Monthly Press, 2004) and John Keegan, *The Face of Battle* (New York: Penguin, 1983) as examples.

10. Gary Klein, *Intuition at Work* (New York: Doubleday, 2003), and Max H. Bazerman and Dolly Chugh, "Decisions Without Blinders," *Harvard Business Review*, January 2006, 88–97.

11. See Paul Rogers and Marcia Blenko, "Who Has the D? How Clear Decision Roles Enhance Organizational Performance," *Harvard Business Review*, January 2006, 53–61, for an excellent discussion of decision rights and roles for others who contribute to decisions.

12. James Surowiecki, *The Wisdom of Crowds* (New York: Doubleday, 2004).

Chapter 5

1. See, for example, John Fine, "When Do You Stop the Presses?" *BusinessWeek*, July 23, 2007, 20.

2. Quite clearly, visionaries did indeed imagine the potential for such data.

3. On credit reporting generally, see, for example, Barbara Whitaker, "How to Mend a Credit Report That's Not Really Broken," *New York Times,* August 1, 2004. This article quotes a US PIRG survey showing that 80 percent of credit reports had mistakes, with 25 percent having serious enough errors that credit could be denied. See Deborah Gage and John McCormick, "Blur," *Baseline,* June 2005, 32–56, for an excellent discussion of accuracy issues at ChoicePoint.

4. I believe that Stan Davis also coined the term *mass customization.*

5. Philip Evans and Thomas S. Wurster refer to unbundling as *deconstruction* in *Blown to Bits* (Boston: Harvard Business School Press, 2000).

6. Stan Davis and Bill Davidson, *2020 Vision* (New York: Simon & Schuster, 1991).

7. John Seely Brown and Paul Duguid, *The Social Life of Information* (Boston: Harvard Business School Press, 2000).

8. I first learned of this work in personal communication with Dr. Godfrey. See also http://money.cnn.com/magazines/fortune/fortune_archive/2004/12/13 /8214248/index.htm

9. Steve Rosenbush, "Guess Who's Coming Up Short," *BusinessWeek,* July 23, 2007, 63.

10. Peter Engardio, Dexter Roberts, Frederik Balfour, and Bruce Einhorn, "Broken China," *BusinessWeek,* July 23, 2007, 41.

11. Support for this claim comes from two lines of reasoning. First, legal efforts to combat piracy continue. See, for example, Eric Pfanner, "Effort to Combat Internet Piracy Gains Strength in France," *New York Times,* December 2, 2007, http://www.nytimes.com/2007/12/03/technology/03piracy.html?pagewanted =print. Second, according to a study conducted by ipoque GmbH, a German vendor, peer-to-peer applications account for between 50 percent and 90 percent of overall Internet traffic in Europe and the Middle East. See "Internet Study 2007," http://www.ipoque.com/media/internet_studies/internet_study _2007. In the United States, Comcast may be slowing peer-to-peer traffic as part of its network management program. See, for example, Peter Svenson, "Comcast Blocks Some Internet Traffic, Associated Press, October 19, 2007, http://www .msnbc.msn.com/id/21376597/.

12. See, for example, the annual reports of both companies for the past several years. From data provided by the Organisation Internationale des Constructeurs d' Automobiles (OICA), I conclude that Ford's worldwide market share declined from 11.8 percent in 1999 to 9.2 percent in 2006. During that same period, Toyota's market share increased from 9.2 percent to 11.8 percent. The worldwide market grew by just over 22 percent during that time. The total number of vehicles sold decreased by 5.6 percent for Ford and increased by 47.1 percent for Toyota.

Chapter 6

1. Michael Hammer, "Reengineering Work: Don't Automate, Obliterate," *Harvard Business Review*, July 1990, 104–112.

2. See Nicholas Negroponte, *Being Digital* (New York: Vintage Books, 1996); Frances Cairncross, *The Death of Distance* (Boston: Harvard Business School Press, 1997); Esther Dyson, *Release 2.0* (New York: Broadway Books, 1997); and Thomas Friedman, *The World Is Flat* (New York: Farrar, Straus, and Giroux, 2006).

3. Evelyn Tarner and David Paget-Brown, *How Financial Institutions Can Tune In to the Advantages of Enterprise Data Management* (Somers, NY: IBM Corporation, 2005), http://www-1.ibm.com/services/us/imc/pdf/g510-6223-financial-institutions.pdf.

4. Purists point out that answers to "Where do I find it?" are really content in the form of metadata. This argument is sound. But metadata is not what most searchers really want. They want the data and information they need to complete an operation, make a decision, and so forth. Thus, I prefer to think of info-mediators as facilitators.

5. Catherine Holahan, "Searching for John Q. Public," *BusinessWeek*, July 30, 2007, 72.

6. Ian Ayres, *Super Crunchers* (New York: Bantam Books, 2007); Thomas H. Davenport and Jeanne G. Harris, *Competing on Analytics: The New Science of Winning* (Boston: Harvard Business School Press, 2007).

7. I believe Jeff Hooper, then at Bell Labs, was the first to make this observation, in the 1980s.

8. John Markoff, "Taking Snooping Further," *New York Times*, February 25, 2006.

9. "What the Nose Knows," *The Economist Technology Quarterly*, March 11, 2006, 18–20.

10. Alastair MacWillson, quoted in Larry Greenemeier, "Hard Target: 10th Annual Global Information Security Survey," *InformationWeek*, July 16, 2007.

11. Quoted in Greenemeier, "Hard Target," 41.

12. John McMillan, *Reinventing the Bazaar* (New York: W.W. Norton, 2002).

Chapter 7

1. I have been studying these issues for at least a decade, and I hope that others, with backgrounds different from my own, join the effort. This chapter is based to some degree on an article I wrote entitled "Barriers to Successful Data Quality Management," *Studies in Communication Sciences* 4, no. 2 (December 2004): 53–68, which reflected my best thinking on these issues at the time.

2. Neil A. Lewis, "Rule Created Legal 'Wall' to Sharing Information," *New York Times*, April 14, 2004.

3. See Niccolo Machiavelli, *The Prince*, translated by W. K. Marriot (London: J.M. Dent & Sons, 1958), and R. G. H. Siu, *The Craft of Power* (Malabar, FL: Robert E. Krieger, 1979).

4. Joost Elffers and Robert Greene, *The 48 Laws of Power* (New York: Penguin Group, 1998).

5. Frank Guess of the University of Tennessee, Mahender Singh of MIT, and I have recently started a research project on this subject.

6. Alan Wernick, personal communication, April 6, 2007.

7. As quoted in James Freeman, "You Have Zero Privacy . . . Get Over It!" Tech Central Station, June 15, 2000, http://www.tcsdaily.com/article.aspx?id=051500C.

8. Privacy Rights Clearinghouse, "A Chronology of Data Breaches Reported Since the ChoicePoint Incident," http://www.privacyrights.org/ar/ChronDataBreaches.htm.

9. Deborah Gage and John McCormick, "Blur," *Baseline,* June 2005, 32–56.

10. Gwen Thomas, personal communication, May 15, 2007.

11. For current, detailed information on recent legislation see the Web site for the Identity Theft Resource Center (http://www.idtheftcenter.org).

12. Brad Stone, "To Curb Identity Theft, Proposal Asks Banks to Disclose Incidents," *New York Times*, March 21, 2007.

13. Michael E. Porter, *Competitive Advantage: Creating and Sustaining Superior Performance* (New York: The Free Press, 1985). In some of my earlier work, I called the data and information flows from supplier to one department and the next and finally to the customer "information chains." The phrase awaits general acceptance.

14. I refer to quality revolutions, not *a* quality revolution, because, according to Blan Godfrey, the larger quality revolution actually unfolded as a series of industry-specific revolutions.

15. Galen Gruman, "Close Fast, Close Smart," *CIO*, February 26, 2007, 36–45.

16. Thomas H. Davenport, *Thinking for a Living* (Boston: Harvard Business School Press, 2005).

17. Ted Friedman, *Gartner Study on Data Quality Shows That IT Still Bears the Burden*, Gartner Report G00137680, February 2006.

18. My best source is a feature on the March 22, 2007, NBC Nightly News. College professors in nearly sixty colleges have banned Wikipedia as a citable source in reports. Too many students trust the information found there without question. There are many other anecdotes. See for example "Johnson criticized for recommending Wikipedia," http://www.guardian.co.uk/technology/2007/apr/11/news.politics.

19. Witold Rybczynski, *One Good Turn: A Natural History of the Screwdriver and the Screw* (London: Simon & Schuster, 2000).

20. John Allen Paulos, *Innumeracy* (New York: Hill and Wang, 2001).

Chapter 8

1. Anthony Bisco, "Outsmarting the Market," *BusinessWeek*, January 22, 2007, 58–63.

2. Clay Dodson, personal communication, February 18, 2008.

3. Maria Villar, personal communication, February 25, 2008.

4. Shell was one of my clients. This case study was developed via a series of conversations in 2007. Shell has approved this write-up.

5. W. Edwards Deming, *Quality, Productivity, and Competitive Position* (Cambridge: MIT Center for Advanced Engineering Study, 1982).

6. Thomas K. Landauer, *The Trouble with Computers* (Cambridge: MIT Press, 1997).

7. Thomas Friedman, "Data Quality 'Firewall' Enhances Value of the Data Warehouse," *CIO Update*, Gartner Research, April 13, 2003.

8. Jeff Averick, personal communication, February 11, 2008.

9. Michael Brackett, *Data Resource Quality: Turning Bad Habits into Good Practices* (Boston: Addison Wesley, 2000).

10. Marianne Kolbasuk McKee, "The Useless Hunt for Data," *Information Week*, January 1/8, 2007, 19.

11. Importantly, different customers have different requirements for finding data. A senior executive might expect to find them among the summary reports that wind their way to his desk every month, a midlevel executive via an intranet portal, and operational employees via an application program. Systems developers may require far greater detail, down to the precise location of a specific value in a database management system.

12. This case study was developed via a series of conversations in 2007. Aera has approved this write-up.

13. Indeed, Alan Wernick recommends that the two levels include something you know (a password) and something you have (a smartcard).

14. This case study was developed via a series of conversations in 2007. JPMorgan has approved this write-up.

15. As of July 18, 2007.

16. I cited Dr. Juran's insights on the needs for senior leadership for quality in chapter 3. Readers may wish to consult Joseph M. Juran, "Made in USA: A Renaissance in Quality," *Harvard Business Review*, July–August 1993, 47.

17. This statement is a rewording of my favorite quality policy of all time.

18. A somewhat more cynical view of this work is that many people resist new thinking, tools, and techniques. One frequent comment is "This doesn't apply to us because . . ." Thus, the work of the CDO aims to mitigate excuses.

19. Nitin Nohria and Robert G. Eccles, eds., *Networks and Organizations* (Boston: Harvard Business School Press, 1992), 197.

20. Albert-Laszlo Barabasi, *Linked: The New Science of Networks* (Cambridge: Perseus Publishing, 2002), 17.

21. Elliott Jacques, *Requisite Organization* (Arlington, VA: Cason Hall, 1996), 75.

Appendix A

1. Frederick Winslow Taylor, *Principles of Scientific Management* (New York: Harper & Row, 1967).

2. Herbert G. Houze and Elizabeth Mankin Kornhauser, *Samuel Colt: Arms, Art and Invention* (New Haven, CT: Yale University Press, 2006).

3. Douglas Brinkley, *Wheels for the World: Henry Ford, His Company, and a Century of Progress* (New York: Viking Books, 2003).

4. Walter A. Shewart, *Economic Control of Quality of Manufactured Product: 50th Anniversary Commemorative Reissue* (Milwaukee: ASQC, 1980).

5. Joesph M. Juran, *Juran on Leadership for Quality: An Executive Handbook* (New York: The Free Press, 1989).

6. W. Edwards Deming, *Quality, Productivity, and Competitive Position* (Cambridge: MIT Press, 1982).

7. Michael Hammer and Richard Champy, *Reengineering the Corporation: A Manifesto for Business Revolution* (New York: Harper Collins, 1993).

8. Thomas H. Davenport, *Thinking for a Living* (Boston: Harvard Business School Press, 2005).

Appendix B

1. The process laboratory could also report to the chief data office.

2. *Webster's New World College Dictionary,* 4th ed. (Foster City, CA: IDG Books Worldwide, 2001).

Appendix C

1. Lisa Myers and the NBC Investigative Unit, "Stolen Military Data for Sale in Afghanistan," NBC Nightly News, April 13, 2006.

2. This definition is based on David C. Hay, *Data Model Patterns: Conventions of Thought* (New York: Dorsett, 1996).

3. David Hay, "What Exactly *Is* a Data Model?" parts 1 to 3, *DM Review*, February, March, and April 2003.

4. *Webster's New World College Dictionary,* 4th ed. (Foster City, CA: IDG Books Worldwide, 2001).

Index

About the Author

Thomas C. Redman ("The Data Doc") helps organizations improve their data and put them to work. He and his wife, Nancy, live in Rumson, New Jersey.